The Test Score Decline

THE TEST SCORE DECLINE
meaning and issues

Lawrence Lipsitz
Editor

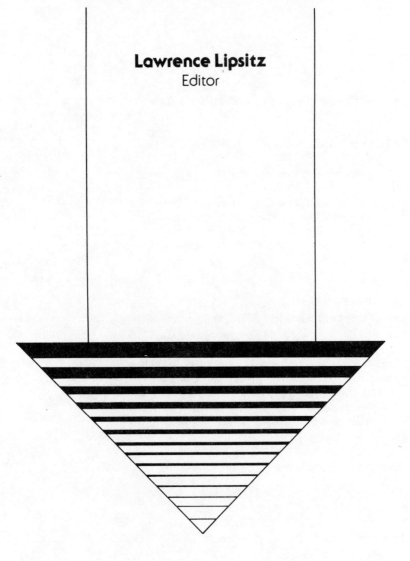

Educational Technology Publications
Englewood Cliffs, New Jersey 07632

Library of Congress Cataloging in Publication Data
Main entry under title:

The Test score decline.

    "First published in the June and July, 1976 issues
of Educational technology."
    1. Educational tests and measurements—United
States—Addresses, essays, lectures. I. Lipsitz,
Lawrence. II. Educational technology.
LB3051.T43   371.2'6'0973   76-13169
ISBN 0-87778-095-1

Printed in the United States of America.

Library of Congress Catalog Card Number:
76-13169.

International Standard Book Number:
0-87778-095-1.

First Printing: January, 1977.

Preface

This collection of original papers, first published in the June and July, 1976 issues of *Educational Technology* Magazine, was prompted by the enormous public outcry which greeted the general public realization that achievement and college aptitude test scores were continuing in recent months and years the steady erosion which began in the mid-1960s.

By the end of 1975, the cumulative effect of decline after decline had become so pronounced that the popular press started to print alarming stories questioning what was happening in the nation's schools. The alarms focused especially on perhaps the most visible and widely known series of tests, the Scholastic Aptitude Test (SAT) administered by Educational Testing Service for the College Entrance Examination Board (CEEB).

Among the questions asked were the following: Is the decline in skills real, or is there something wrong with the tests? If the decline *is* real, then what accounts for it? Are the schools falling down on their job? Are the youth of the nation becoming progressively more incompetent in basic intellectual skills, including reading and mathematics?

The controversy arose at a time of widespread questioning of all American institutions, including the public schools. Calls for greater accountability and more cost-effective approaches to instruction, which have been made with increasing fervor during the past few years, increased with the evidence that test scores were going down; therefore, it was said increasingly, the schools *must* be doing a poor job, despite all the billions of dollars spent on improvement projects during the past two decades.

Countless theories and speculations were advanced by laymen and educators alike to account for the decline—or to state reasons why the apparent decline was not really a decline, after all.

Amid this controversy, the Editors of *Educational Technology* decided to commission a series of papers by a cross-section of informed persons working in the field of education to clarify what had been taking place in the schools and in achievement testing, and to attempt to point the way toward a resolution of this latest "crisis" in American education.

While an eminent Commission had been appointed by the CEEB to look into the same area, it was decided that it was important to try to arrive at some clarification of the issues well in advance of the projected 1978 conclusion of the Commission's research study; and it was thought that this timely series of articles might indeed be helpful to the Commission itself as it went about its work.

The authors of the present papers are to be complimented for their willingness to take on this writing task in view of the unsettled nature of the situation. Indeed, writing at this early date, one risks the chance of being proved "wrong" as more data are accumulated through the passage of time. Many authors, of course, are not so intellectually courageous; they do not take positions until after all the facts are known and digested, when the issue becomes "safe." By writing when they did, the authors of the following papers have helped all of us to understand the issues involved in the test score controversy, and to hasten the day when definitive answers will be available to many, if not most, of the questions being asked about the decline in test scores.

Lawrence Lipsitz
November, 1976

Table of Contents

The Test Score Decline

1.

The Marrow of Achievement
Test Score Declines

Annegret Harnischfeger and
David E. Wiley

After two decades of educational reform and innovation, there is now emerging a strong movement toward restoration: Back to the fundaments of traditional schooling. This movement is nourished by resource cutbacks often resulting in instructional curtailment, but also by alarming news of achievement test score declines. The common view seems to be that if the declines are real, something is wrong with American Education, and that the way to correct this condition is curricular reconstruction: Back to Basics!

1. Some Facts About
Test Score Changes

The apparent facts about achievement changes, as exhibited in the media, in research reports and on the occasion of conferences focusing on achievement measurement, curriculum and school administration, are the following. Since the mid-1960s, declines have occurred in these tests:

- *Scholastic Aptitude Test*. SAT scores (11th and 12th grade) have dropped for males and females in both verbal and mathematical sections.
- *American College Tests*. ACT scores (11th and 12th

Annegret Harnischfeger and **David E. Wiley** are with the ML-GROUP for Policy Studies in Education, CEMREL, Inc., 875 N. Michigan Avenue, Chicago, Illinois.

grade) have dropped in English, mathematics and social science for males and females.

- *Minnesota Scholastic Aptitude Test.* High school junior test scores (11th grade) have declined.
- *Iowa Tests of Educational Development.* ITED scores have declined in all areas for grades 9 through 12 in the State of Iowa.
- *Iowa Tests of Basic Skills.* ITBS national norm data indicate drops in language, mathematics and reading. State of Iowa data from grades 5 through 8 show declines in all areas.
- *Comprehensive Tests of Basic Skills.* CTBS national norm data show declines in mathematics and reading from grade 5 and language from grade 6 through 10.
- *National Assessment of Educational Progress.* NAEP data show declines in science at each age level and in writing at ages 13 and 17.

No trends have been found in these:

- ACT Science test (11th and 12th grade).
- *Preliminary Scholastic Aptitude Test* (PSAT: 11th grade).
- ITBS State of Iowa data for grade 4.
- CTBS national norm data for grade 5 reading, and language in grades 3 and 5.

Increases have been detected in these:

- NAEP literacy for 17-year-olds and writing for 9-year-olds.
- ITBS State of Iowa data for grade 3 in all areas.
- CTBS national norm data for grades 2 and 4 in reading, language and mathematics, and grade 3 in reading and mathematics.
- *Stanford-Binet.* Norming data between the 1930s and 1972 show a dramatic rise.
- *Metropolitan Readiness Tests.* These scores have risen for pre-first-graders.

Generally, through the 1940s, 1950s and up to the mid-1960s, achievement test scores steadily increased. Since then, scores have been declining in all tested achievement areas for grades 5 through 12, with more dramatic drops occurring in recent years and being most evident for higher grades. The declines have been most pronounced in verbal tests and therein for college-bound females. There is no evidence for declines at younger ages and in lower grades (grades 1, 2, 3 and 4), but perhaps there are increases. It is noteworthy that today's first-graders enter school with more developed skills, as measured by readiness tests, than their counterparts of the mid-1960s (Mitchell, 1974). Definitely, children now enter first grade with more knowledge of letter names and word meaning, and also more knowledge about numbers. Our analyses indicate that these findings are real, not artifacts, and that they describe a national phenomenon.[1] And this great generality of the phenomenon draws our concern.

Some of the specifics of the declines provide provocative ground for more complex interpretations than those commonly advanced. The fact that achievements measured in higher grades have declined more than those measured in lower ones reflects differences in content tested as well as the ages of the test-takers. For example, large declines have generally been observed in most verbal-oriented tests, except those given in the lower and middle elementary grades. However, the latter primarily measure decoding, word-structure, basic vocabulary and simple comprehension skills, i.e., literacy, while the tests used in later grades are oriented toward comprehension and interpretation of more complex textual materials. The only increases in verbal skills that were found for higher grades (11th and 12th; National Assessment of Educational Progress, in 1975) correspond to those simpler skills measured by standardized tests in elementary school. One straightforward interpretation would be that "basic" reading skills are increasing but more advanced ones are declining. As the grade-level discrepancy in achievement-score trend holds more generally, not merely for verbal-related skills, interpretation of those results must give heed to test content.

2. Have Compositions of the Tests
or the Test-Takers Changed?

In evaluating the findings, our first explanatory attempt concerned the measurement instruments that showed the declining score trends. But we soon had to conclude that changes in scoring, scaling, testing conditions or test content could not explain the large achievement decreases. We did not pinpoint any content changes in tests. A limited formal assessment was made by longitudinally comparing categories of test items for one test (SAT) over time, but less formal assessments were performed for other tests. In general, test content changes might have to take responsibility for slight score changes, but they can definitely not explain the general phenomenon. Some non-content, technical changes in tests worked in the opposite direction. For example, we found that changes in two tests (SAT, PSAT) had resulted in scaling increases. Thus, accounting for these would even augment the magnitudes of achievement test score declines.

The other immediately obtruding possible *explicans* for the achievement score drops is change in the test-taking student population. And, in fact, Munday (1976) in a report on college-bound students claims that the large score drops for college-bound females are due to the greater number of less skilled females now entering college. This actually might explain part of the more severe verbal score declines for females. Another achievement-relevant factor often advanced to explain the declines among the college-bound is the socioeconomic status of test takers. We need to explore the likelihood of a decrease in the socioeconomic level of those taking college entrance examinations. However, these changes, and those in the entering college population generally, cannot account for the decline.[2] The portion of college entrants coming from upper income families (over $15,000; constant 1973 dollars) increased 17 percent (from 41.3 to 48.2 percent) from 1967 to 1973, while those with lower income increased only about 8 percent (from 6.7 to 7.3 percent). Middle income families decreased their representation 14 percent (from 52.0 to 44.5 percent). Over-all, the median income of college students' families rose 8.9 percent (from $13,481 to $14,679). Thus, if scores of each socioeconomic group had remained constant, the average scores of all college entrants would have *increased* due to compositional effects, given the known relation between socioeconomic status and achievement.

Compositional changes of test-takers have been brought about in grades 5 through 12 by a sharp decrease in pupil dropout rate, which has been especially pronounced for higher grade levels. From 1950 to 1968 the pupil dropout rate fell from 50 to 25 percent.[3] Since then it has been stable. This fact implies that considerably greater numbers of pupils who a decade ago would have dropped out of school, and therefore not taken tests, are now in fact taking tests. These students typically are in the lower achievement ranges and might thus account for a part of the general achievement decline.

Another factor being held responsible for achievement score declines for 12th graders is the states' policy trends of easing early graduation. The argument is that these policies result in creaming off the high achievers. Actually, early high school graduation has increased nationwide (Educational Research Service, 1975) from 2.2 percent (1971-72) to 7.7 percent (1973-74). However, the data indicate that early graduating pupils represent most of the spectrum of high school pupils except the lowest ranges of achievement, and this has not changed. Definitely, there is little overrepresentation of college entrants. Thus, the relatively large achievement score declines for 12th graders cannot be explained by a cream-off effect of early graduators.

Although slight portions of achievement score decreases might be attributable to factors inherent in test developments and to distributional changes of test takers, the extent of the decline, both with respect to magnitude and consistency, over the past 10 years demands further analysis in order to clarify possible implications for educational policy. Efforts must be made to strengthen conclusions about the extents, locations and types of declines.

We have avoided estimating precise amounts of decline or change. Characterizing precise magnitudes in achievement test score trends not only necessitates further research assessing drifts in scaling and composition changes of test takers, but also evaluating other, probably more potent, factors yet to be discussed. It further demands the assessment of content correspondences among instruments and the comparable scaling of content-similar tests.

We are not in the position of attaching quantitative labels to the various factors to which test score changes might be attributable. But we are able to assess grossly the likely potencies that some forces might have in explaining the achievement decline. Definitely, further research should analyze and attempt to attribute precise amounts of test score changes to relevant factors. However, that is merely one step in answering the more important questions of what skills do test scores represent and which of these have declined? E.g., does the large decline in verbal scales indicate less vocabulary or literature knowledge, or fewer conceptual skills? To evaluate and valuate achievement test scores, we will have to find the answers to this type of question.

So, if we conclude that only a minor amount of the test score decline can be attributed to changes in test construction (i.e., test content, scaling) and the composition of test takers, then most of the decline has to have been effected by changes in school, family and society.

3. The Role of the Schools

Naturally, achievement test score declines have, without any deliberation, been valued negatively, and blame has been immediately thrown on schools and teachers. But also television and societal changes, such as broken families, working mothers and drugs, have been cited as responsible.

The reported achievement declines are presently being taken to support or initiate diverse movements. A considerable number of schools and districts are moving "back to basics," and districts and states are establishing minimal requirements for graduation from elementary and secondary schools. Groups claim on the same data basis either a necessity for more resources in education or, in opposition, try to justify resource cutbacks, claiming that the last decade's increased educational expenditure did not pay off. All of these actions and claims lack ground, as, so far, more expert and intensive attempts at attribution (or scapegoating) have failed. More thinking, analysis and research are required before grounded action or reasoned policies can be recommended. And we should be prepared in our process of research evaluation and valuation of the last decade's achievement score declines to find a multifaceted array of decline-relevant factors that is not easily translatable into action plans.

The likely potentiality and the relative ease of intervenability tempted us to first search for factors allowing the attribution of achievement decreases to the school. And therein, curricula, course taking, length of school year and day, absences, desegregation, teaching staff characteristics and attitudes toward learning seemed viable for assessing the meaning of the achievement declines.

Curriculum, one fundamental characteristic of education, is often ignored by those concerned with the interpretation of test scores: What is *learned* depends strongly on what is *taught*. Differences in educational quality or efficiency contribute to the rapidity with which children move through a curriculum, but when curricula are diverse, children will learn different things. Curricular diversity is thus reflected in the levels of achievement exhibited by tests. That is, one of the strongest contributors to the test-specific pupil achievement ought to be the curriculum. Curriculum in this sense refers to the content that is actually taught in the schools. It varies often within the school, from school to school and district to district, as well as, of course, over grade levels. Curricula vary in their goals and objectives, in teaching methods, in materials, in course and instructional organization, in sequencing and in timing of instruction.

Standardized tests are constructed so as to take many of these features into account. The item-selection process might hold one key to the understanding of test score declines. Typical resources for goal analysis involved in item-selection are state and local curricular guides and curricular materials. Items are developed from different curricula across the United States, and their norms are derived from national samples of pupils in the relevant age and grade ranges.

This item-selection process boldly assumes a match of guidelines, textbooks and other materials with actual teaching. It is worthwhile asking to what extent this has been or is the case. What we do know is that when basic curricula drastically change, as with the introduction of the "new math," tests fundamentally change so as to not result in "artificial" achievement declines in the test content aligned to former curricula.

Unfortunately, direct evidence of curricular changes in United States schools is difficult to discover. Neither federal agencies, responsible for educational data collection, nor interest groups (such as the NEA) have seen fit to regularly collect data on this important aspect of schooling. We actually do not know how closely tests match what is taught in the schools.

If we find that tests and curricular goals match less nowadays than a decade ago, then the relevance of the achievement test score decline would be restricted to the matching parts of tests and curricula. If, however, we discover that present curricula and tests address the same goals, then we ought to be able to detect other factors responsible for lowered achievements. It is mandatory therefore to assess the likely congruence of tests and instruction.

The view conveyed here distinguishes among curricular goals, implemented curricula and achievement test results. If tests are to be used to validly inform us about what is learned in the schools, then they must be interpreted in terms of their matches to the desired goals and to the educative activities taking place. Otherwise, they cannot enlighten us about the relation between teaching and learning.

Some gross, indirect evidence of curricular change, the nearest approximations to direct curricular evidence available, can be drawn from data for secondary-school course enrollments by subject area. The National Center for Education Statistics has available survey data on the average numbers of courses taken by secondary pupils in various curricular areas from 1948-49 to 1972-73 (*The Condition of Education*, 1975). The data are spotty in their coverage, intermediate school years being only 1960-61 and 1970-71. Generally, the average numbers of courses were constant for the two earliest years, higher in the 1970-71 sample, and dropped again by 1972-73. It is unclear when the decline in course taking began. The peak could have occurred during any of the school years between 1961 and 1971. However, there was clearly a large drop between 1970-71 and 1972-73. In this period, also during which achievement declines occurred, the average number of courses per pupil dropped by 13 percent. These gross numbers are difficult to interpret, however, because they do not indicate what kinds of courses were taken. Fortunately, refined data are available for 1970-71 and 1972-73, so we can discuss some of the details of more recent short-term curricular changes (Gertler and Barker, 1972; Osterndorf, 1975).

Some large changes occurred over the two-year period in the proportions of pupils enrolled in each grade from 7 through 12 who were also taking general grade-specific English courses. The proportion of course-enrolled pupils decreased at every grade level. This drop is substantial, averaging about 15 percent over all grade levels. The over-all percentages of secondary pupils (grades 7-12) enrolled in other (neither general nor grade-specific) English courses has increased over the two-year period. However, these enrollment increases by no means balance the decreases in regular, general English courses.

The total proportion of all secondary pupils enrolled in regular courses declined from 88.7 percent to 75.2 percent, a drop of 15.2 percent,[4] while the enrollment in other courses only increased 5.2 percent (from .517 to .544 courses per pupil). A total drop of almost 8 percent in total English enrollments (from 1.405 to 1.296 courses per pupil) in a two-year period is a probable and startling cause of verbal score declines.

A similar picture emerges in foreign language enrollments. While junior high school enrollments have remained stable at 4.6 percent of total secondary course enrollments, there has been an enrollment decline of 7.5 percent in high school foreign languages (from .199 to .184 courses per pupil). The largest declines have occurred in French (-14 percent), with only marginally smaller drops in German (-13 percent) and Latin (-13 percent). Spanish enrollments, on the other hand, have slightly increased, by 2.6 percent (from .115 to .118). The decreases have been relatively greater (-25 percent) in less popular languages, total course enrollments dropping from .012 to .009 courses per pupil over this period. The most sizable drops have occurred in high school first-year language courses (-9 percent), followed by second-year course enrollments (-7.5 percent). Enrollments in more advanced courses have shown the smallest decline (-3 percent).

History enrollments have not shown any sizable drop (-0.6 percent), diminishing from .507 to .504 courses per pupil. However, they have redistributed markedly. Regular history course taking has declined 6 percent (from .438 to .412), with the largest drops occurring in U.S. History (-7 percent) and State History (-14.5 percent). World History has not substantially altered in popularity. By level, the greatest decrease in regular history enrollments took place in junior (-10 percent) rather than senior high school (-4 percent). Elective and specialized courses took up the slack from these declines, increasing by 33 percent (from .069 to .092 courses per pupil) over the two-year period.

Mathematics enrollments show an interesting pattern of change. Remedial math taking increased by more than 80 percent (1.4 to 2.6 percent) while enrollments in general mathematics decreased 15 percent (41.1 to 34.8 percent). Traditional college preparatory mathematics (algebra, geometry, trigonometry) remained approximately constant (12.4 to 12.8 percent), drops in algebra being compensated by increases in more advanced areas. And other mathematics (mostly advanced) increased by about one-third from 2.8 to 3.7 percent. In aggregate, these changes imply that the total number of courses per pupil in mathematics decreased from 0.768 to 0.713, a total drop in enrollment of more than 7 percent in two years. Again, curricular change is a likely strong influence on tested achievements in mathematics.

With respect to natural science curricula, there has been a large drop in secondary enrollments in general science (-13 percent, from 25.2 to 21.9 percent), especially in senior high school, where the decline reached 30 percent (from 9.2 to 6.4 percent). In the specific sciences, enrollments in the regular first-year courses offered in high schools have suffered the most systematic deterioration (biology: -1 percent, from 14.8 to 14.6 percent; chemistry: -10 percent, from 6.0 to 5.4 percent; physics: -30 percent, from 3.3 to 2.3 percent), the decline increasing with more stringent mathematical prerequisites.

On the other hand, there has been an increase in total high school enrollments in the biological sciences (+15 percent, from 19.9 to 22.8 percent), but these increases have occurred solely through advanced and specialty courses (+61 percent, from 5.1 to 8.2 percent). In the physical sciences, advanced and specialized enrollments have remained essentially constant (-0.7 percent, from 14.9 to 14.8 percent), implying an over-all course enrollment drop in physical science of 7 percent.

Finally, the question arises: If there are such drops in academic course taking, have there been corresponding increases in more practical course enrollments? The answer to this appears to be a resounding NO! Courses for practical training (e.g., vocational, business, home economics) dropped more than 30 percent over the two-year period.

These data present a general picture of the developments which have taken place from 1970-71 to 1972-73 in American secondary curricula as they have been implemented in the schools:

- There has been a general enrollment drop in academic courses.

- This general decline has come about mostly because of substantial decreases in general course taking which have not been substantially replaced by increases in elective or specialty courses.
- There has been a sizable drop in the proportions of pupils enrolling in the traditional basic courses of the college preparatory curricula: algebra, first-year foreign language, chemistry and physics.
- There have been no sizable declines in advanced college preparatory courses. It is not clear whether this was due to stable basic enrollments of those who traditionally take advanced work, or whether the enrollment drops in more basic courses had not yet reached advanced levels.
- Additionally, there have been extreme drops in more practical courses giving preparation for employment and homemaking.
- We lack information on what pupils' activities have changed *to*. Possible factors are: lowered instructional offerings and increasing work-study programs not accounted as courses.

These course enrollment declines parallel closely the test score decline patterns. Declines both in course enrollment and achievement scores are largest for English, followed by mathematics and natural sciences. The one test (ACT) that had stable science scores and the sharp decline in the national science assessment also parallel the stable enrollments for advanced science courses, taken by college-bound students, and the sharp decline in basic natural science course enrollments, intended for typical high school students.

What does the enrollment decline in basic secondary courses indicate? Definitely, pupils are taking fewer courses in most curricular areas. And the redistribution pattern of courses actually taken indicates a shift away from standard courses and traditional academic courses toward specialty and elective courses. These facts raise a host of questions: Are fewer secondary schools offering traditional courses? Or, are fewer pupils enrolling in offered courses? Or both? How are decisions made about enrollment and are the factors which strongly influence secondary pupils' choices different than they used to be? What makes Johnny take algebra? Has the lowered pay-off of college education extended its influence to secondary school? Have parents become less interested in their children's education?

In spite of all these unanswered questions, one clear inference is that typical students are less exposed to traditional basic courses. If, therefore, achievement tests centrally focus on these goals, typically addressed in basic courses, we would expect a score decline. Another viable question, however, concerns shifts in goal emphasis, i.e., the goals that students still are expected to reach as compared to those that now receive less stress. Total test scores do not reveal that selection process; only content-based item analyses would yield this highly important information.

Collatorally, we have detected some increase in elective courses. An important question is: Which goals of those courses are tests now representing? Elective course diversity is large, which makes test coverage of goals difficult. The extent to which such goals are reflected in current achievement tests warrants investigation. So, independent of the question of what goals *should* be attained, we have to analyze the match between goals addressed in school and goals tested. Any valuation of test score declines has to perform this analysis.

We would like to strongly emphasize this necessity by pointing to two results: (1) A study of curricular evaluations by Walker and Schaffarzick (1974) indicates that when achievement tests are aligned to the goals of an innovative curriculum, it generally out-performed rival curricula. However, when more traditional tests are used, the traditional curricula, to which the new one was compared, produce higher scores. (2) A number of school districts startled by declining achievement test scores have taken immediate action toward back-to-basics, meaning restoration of traditional obligatory basic courses, often accompanied by revival of long-forgotten disciplinary rules, including dress codes. A sizable number of these districts and schools claim that they have reversed the declining achievement score trend.

We cited these occurrences to pinpoint the crucial character of the curriculum-test match and to caution the reader away from short-circuited inferences. So far, we only certified that some of what used to be learned is not learned any more. We neither know, at other than a general level, what it is that pupils are not learning any more, nor do we know what they might be learning that is not tested.

The back-to-basics movement clearly reflects curricular change. Sales of instructional equipment are dropping, while those of textbooks with more traditional content emphasis are rising. This development does not, however, merely reflect a change in curricular emphasis. The whole notion of "basic" skills or, more generally, "basic" education is fundamentally homogenizing. It implies that there is an underlying foundation of skills or learnings which precurse subsequent, more diverse, learnings. Whether these are conceived as psychologically prerequisite or socially mandatory is irrelevant to their homogenizing character. Under either conception they are exhibited as a primary common component of the curriculum. Consequently, the greater the emphasis on (the more instructional time devoted to) such basics, the more similar are the educative experiences of individuals.

The back-to-basics movement counters one important characteristic of recent curricular trends: The increase in the diversity of offered and accepted experiences, at least in secondary school. This trend has exhibited itself in (1) the increasing local diversity of curricula, (2) the augmented numbers of courses appealing to special groups and (3) the greater numbers of elective as opposed to "core" courses.

It is, of course, much easier to representatively assess the state of intended learnings when the curricula have a large common core of "basics" than when they have little commonality. If we have moved from an era when tests were developed against the background of strong consensus on goals, and consequent great similarity in the curricula widely offered, to an era of disagreement over goals and curricular diversity, but little change in test coverage, then achievement declines on standardized tests would naturally follow. In fact, it is hard to see, under these conditions, how scores could not drop.

Problematically, the back-to-basics movement seems to neglect the untested content in only focusing on skills that are commonly represented in most tests. Has the movement's reemphasis on educational fundamentals been simplistically derived from test score declines, together with other dissatisfactions, such as increased societal permissiveness, or has it resulted from a thorough reconsideration of educational goals and the curriculum? For a thoughtful and engaged educator, it is at this time difficult to endorse the movement. What we need, and what the achievement score trends should provoke, is a reconsideration and debate over educational goals.

While secondary schools have undergone tremendous diversification—high school consolidation, career education, cultural and ethnic group considerations all have nourished this development—it is likely that elementary schools have more intensively concentrated on "basics." Enormous amounts of federal funds have been focused on reading, writing and arithmetic, especially in the lower elementary grades. And, actually, test scores up to grade 4 indicate rising rather than declining achievement. It is worth considering whether the focus on basics in those grades and the close match of tests and curricular goals are responsible for this achievement picture. The picture is further confused by the increase in pre-first grade readiness scores, cited above. We have little understanding of these issues, as we completely lack data that would enlighten the inside of elementary school.

Our ignorance about our schools is astounding, and this in a country where more data collection, assessment and evaluation are taking place than anywhere else. Besides the crude and simplified course enrollment data for secondary schools, no nationwide data on content of teaching and learning are available. We definitely should be more informed about school education, as this is the society's most important investment.

Although we do know that the length of the school year over the last decade has typically been about 180 days, we only suspect from scattered survey data that there must be large variation in the length of the school day. No nationwide statistics are available.

A factor that might be related to achievement test score trends is pupil absence rate, which has steadily increased over the past decade, resulting in smaller average amounts of schooling for pupils, but also burdening the teaching process considerably.

A factor to be positively valued, although it might be responsible for part of the *evident* test score declines, is pupil dropout rate (see 2.) which, in 1968, stabilized at an all-time low (25 percent). Considerably more dropout-prone—and typically low achieving—pupils now continue schooling until graduation. We should not undervalue this as a possible cause of manifest test score decline, even though it may signal increases in general academic accomplishment.

Have pupils changed in their assessment of the importance of schooling to their future lives? If so, this could have important effects on how much and what they choose to learn and on how seriously they take those testing situations used to assess their accomplishments. Lower pupil motivation might follow from the now generally lower pay-off of education in our society. Data supporting an economic view of education are the lower college enrollment figures for students of middle income families (see 2.). But we might also conceive that pupil motivation for learning, especially for traditional academic areas, could decrease as a consequence of more general societal movements favoring emotional, religious, expressive and aesthetic issues over academic or predominantly cognitive aspects. Presently, we lack empirical evidence on motivational changes of pupils, although lowered motivation for school and learning is an often heard complaint from teachers and parents.

Pupil mobility or desegregation seem not to have any explanatory power, as regional and state differences contradict the widespread character of the declines.

Teaching staff characteristics such as experience and education are possible distal causes, but existing data do not reveal any evidence for their playing a relevant role in the current test score drops.

Also, for some of the factors connected to school reorganization in the past decade, such as continuing high school consolidation and the crowded state of elementary schools following the post-war baby-boom, we could not draw any straightforward conclusion of powerful determination of decreasing achievement test scores. This difficulty arises from the simultaneity of their accompaniment by massive funding increases and the inconsistency of their likely impact with grade-level differences in the decline.

The school, however important, is but one agent in educating and socializing children. It is prominent as its mission is defined as primarily educative and developmental, and does not include leisure work, or participation in societal efforts. Politically, the school is most relevant, as it can be used instrumentally both to support or counteract social trends and to achieve new societal goals.

4. Societal Changes

We must consider pupils' out-of-school experiences for two reasons: First, definitely, much learning relevant to academic achievement takes place outside of school and, therefore, we have to look for changes in these contributory experiences of children. Second, the syntony of school and non-school learning will determine if important achievements have been neglected or whether children are paralyzed by inconsistencies in their in- and out-of-school life. Efforts to avoid the latter can be seen in the school's taking charge of many issues that earlier were considered to be the family's responsibility, such as health and sex education, home economics, etc.

The effects of school extend into the pupil's out-of-school social life also as schools frame the opportunities for social activity and personal interaction. They determine the availability of friendships, and initiate most activities—including highly problematic ones such as drug and alcohol consumption—merely via the amount of time that peer groups are required to spend together.

The National Institute on Drug Abuse (NIDA) reports that 8- to 14-year-olds constitute the fastest growing group of drug users. It has been estimated that 20 percent of pupils older than 11 years have tried marijuana and that about 6 percent of high school seniors smoke it and/or drink alcohol daily (Holden, 1975). Another indicator of non-compliance with societal norms is the recently reported and alarming increase in youth crime. Are youths indifferent to traditional societal values and achievement goals? We don't know. Certainly this issue needs clarification in understanding achievement test score declines.

Television is often assigned a core function in altering pupil experiences over the past 25 years. The main arguments are that it decreases the time that was otherwise devoted to homework and reading and that it impoverishes family interaction. We did not discover or retrieve any data enlightening this issue. The only evidence we found indicates that, in fact, set ownership and the amount of time that families spend viewing television has continually increased since 1950, including the period of the test score decline (Bower, 1973). But to be of any evidential significance, we would need to know what and how long children of various ages view television. Is it likely (1) that the general visual and verbal stimulation of television and the existence of educative pre-school programs are responsible for the achievement increases in lower grades, and (2) that older children's television viewing has a contrary effect—keeping them from educationally important activities, such as reading or consultative interaction with adults? No data are available.

Clearly, the American family has undergone dramatic changes

over the past 25 years (1945-1974; Bronfenbrenner, 1975). Some educationally important indicators are:

- the increase of labor force participation of married women with school-aged children, from 26 to 51 percent;
- the increase of single parent families, from about 10 to almost 17 percent of all families;
- the 50 percent drop in the proportion of extended families; and
- the tripling of illegitimate children.

These trends seem startling, but as we are not able to concretely relate these societal factors to achievement, we limit ourselves to merely listing them. Composed and configured to a comprehensive and differential picture of changes in the American family, they might well demonstrate relevance for the explanation of declining test scores.

But there are still other family- and generation-specific factors that might relate to achievement declines. The pupil population of the last decade, now in secondary schools, is the baby-boom generation. This pupil generation did not only crowd schools, but also had an unusual family environment. Their parents typically married and had children at a considerably earlier age than parents in the periods before or after (Whelpton, Campbell and Patterson, 1966). This implies, since income increases with age, that those children were, on the average, born into economically poorer environments. A hypothesis we have not yet been able to confirm concerns the likely higher proportion of children born during that time to lower as compared to middle classes. Both historic occurrences might contribute to present test score declines. But there is a third unique feature to that generation, relevant to achievement: childspacing. Children were also born relatively closer to each other in time. Research indicates that, in general, close spacing seems to have negative effects on achievement (Breland, 1974; Zajonc, 1976). Reasons proposed to explain this finding circle around the decreased amount of

individual parental attention or interaction that children receive
when siblings are close in age. However, we lack direct evidence of
the relation of these societal changes to achievement test score
changes. We, therefore, have to remain very speculative about
those potential causes of test score declines located in the society
and more intimately in the family.

5. Implications of Score Declines:
Some Cautions

Beyond doubt, beyond differences among and alterations in
assessment instruments, or in test-takers' compositions, achievement scores have been declining for about a decade in all grades
from grade 5 upwards. Score declines are more pronounced in
higher grades and in recent years, and they are more severe for
tests probing verbal than mathematics achievements. These are the
facts and they describe a national phenomenon.

There is no sole and solitary cause for declining achievement
test scores. Several factors have differentially contributed to the
decline, and their precise assessment is hampered by complex
interrelations. Our analysis served mostly to point toward some
possibly productive research areas, giving priority to areas which
are more tractable politically.

The factors discussed which mostly concern changes in the
family and general society seem to be more distal to the decline
issue, and most of them have little political potency. We,
therefore, abstain from encouraging extensive research in those
areas as a means of clarifying the relevance of political actions to
the test score decline issue. These are more commonly located
within the school context.

In the school arena, one important issue is the consequence
for manifest achievement test score declines of the drastically
lower pupil dropout rate. We need to know the extent to which
distributional changes are due to the test participation of types of
pupils who used to drop out before the mid-1960s. And we need
to clarify the distributions of absences, over grades, for different

types of pupils. This research is, in substance, closely related to the elucidation of possible changes in pupils' learning motivation.

We reported lowered test scores in diverse areas: English, writing, literature, vocabulary, reading, social studies, mathematics and natural sciences. These are traditional academic learning areas. What are the typical accomplishments in these areas that are assessed by standardized tests? And where are the deficiencies? Are they losses in knowledge, concept formation, abstraction, analytic skills. . .? Only thoughtful content analyses of tests can answer this important question. We also need to ask whether pupils have gained in areas not assessed with typical standardized tests: Have they improved in effectiveness of public debate and speech? Have they gained in human understanding or aesthetic issues (art, music)? Have there been relevant curricular changes?

The trend in secondary education toward "special" and more expressive courses indicates that the traditional common academic base may not be readily accepted anymore, either by teachers or by pupils, as course offerings and enrollments hint. Maybe parts of traditional course contents are obsolete, and perhaps instead of attempting innovation of traditional curricula, which is a cumbersome and expensive process, the practical education community has been helping itself with new "special" courses, whose contents might be highly distinctive from school to school and not attended to by test developers.

For example, do the changes in history course-taking, moving from State and American History toward World History and special courses (including Black History), indicate a due revision of traditional history offerings? Does the move toward "special" courses in English, such as science fiction and media analysis, necessitate a reconsideration of what basic courses should contain? Are academic courses with stress on future long-term intellectual and economic benefits, especially in a time of lowered educational pay-offs, losing out to courses allowing more short-term satisfactions and immediate gratification? What are the changes in out-of-school learnings? And what do test developments pick up?

It seems that the call for "back to basics" is unfounded in that it is not based on thorough reconsiderations of what is and should be learned in school. Instead of rethinking educational goals and calling for matching, goal-unfolding assessment instruments, this movement seems to blindly adhere to an authority named "test," which is nothing but a means for assessing and evaluating actual educational outcomes against predefined educational goals.

Definitely, curricular changes are highly likely to be responsible for part of the test score decline. But we also need to clarify what lower academic course enrollments mean. Other systematic changes, including declines in vocational and music enrollments and increases in artistic ones, make the general pattern difficult to understand. Are these decreases indicators for shortened school days, or increased study halls which substitute for homework? If not, to what extent are these courses replaced—beyond the small increases in special offerings—by aesthetic or expressive activities, or vocational pursuits not categorized as courses, such as work-study programs or increases in part-time jobs?

We need to valuate losses and possible gains in pupils' knowledges and skills responsibly against a thoughtful vision of our, but mainly their, future. The recent test score declines should initiate a reconsideration of basic and advanced skills, skills necessary for a rounded life, consumption, employment, leisure and political action. The importance of achievement test score declines can not be meaningfully assessed—and thoughtful action can not be initiated—without a thorough consideration of these issues and questions.

References

Bower, R.T. *Television and the Public.* New York: Holt, Rinehart and Winston, 1973.

Breland, H.M. Birth Order, Family Configuration, and Verbal Achievement. *Child Development,* 1974, *45,* 1011-1019.

Bronfenbrenner, U. The Next Generation of Americans. Paper presented for the Annual Meeting of the American Association of Advertising Agencies. Dorado, Puerto Rico, March 1975.

Educational Research Service. Early Graduation from High School: Policy and Practice. *ERS Report.* Arlington, Virginia: Educational Research Service, 1975.

Gertler, D.B. and L.A. Barker. *Patterns of Course Offerings and Enrollments in Public Secondary Schools, 1970-71.* DHEW Publication No. (OE) 74-11400. Washington, D.C.: U.S. Government Printing Office, 1972.

Harnischfeger, A. and D.E. Wiley. *Achievement Test Score Decline: Do We Need to Worry?* St. Louis, Mo.: CEMREL, Inc., 1975.

Holden, C. Drug Abuse 1975: The "War" Is Past, the Problem Is as Big as Ever. *Science*, November 1975, *190*(14), 638-641.

Mitchell, B.C. Changes Over an Eight- and a Nine-Year Period in the Readiness Level of Entering First-Grade Pupils. Paper presented at the Annual Meeting of the National Council on Measurement in Education, Chicago, April 1974.

Munday, L.A. *Declining Admissions Test Scores.* ACT Research Report No. 71. Iowa City, Iowa: American College Testing Program, 1976.

Osterndorf. L. *Summary of Offerings and Enrollments in Public Secondary Schools, 1972-73.* DHEW Publication No. (NCES) 76-150. Washington, D.C.: U.S. Government Printing Office, 1975.

U.S. Department of Health, Education and Welfare, National Center for Education Statistics. *The Condition of Education.* Washington, D.C.: U.S. Government Printing Office, 1975.

Walker, D.F. and J. Schaffarzick. Comparing Curricula. *Review of Educational Research*, 1974, *44*, 83-111.

Whelpton, P.K., A.A. Campbell and J.E. Patterson. *Fertility and Family Planning in the United States.* Princeton, N.J.: Princeton University Press, 1966.

Zajonc, R.B. Family Configuration and Intelligence. *Science*, April 1976, *191*(16), 227-236.

Notes

1. For a detailed discussion of these achievement test score changes and analyses of possible causes, see Harnischfeger and Wiley, 1975.
2. The socioeconomic compositions of groups of, e.g., SAT-takers, has been almost identical to the corresponding college entrants.
3. High school dropouts per 1,000 students entering 5th grade.
4. The drop of 15.2 percent is calculated on the base of 88.7 percent in 1970-71. I.e., $-0.152 = \dfrac{75.2 - 88.7}{88.7}$

This figure represents the relative drop in the proportion of those enrolled over the two-year period. This mode of calculating percentages is also used for the curricular areas which follow. Also note that these figures are actually number of courses per pupil. Only when pupils are not likely to take more than one course do we refer to percentages.

The authors assume joint and equal responsibility for this work. David E. Wiley is on leave from the University of Chicago. Preparation of this article was partially supported by the Ford Foundation. Views expressed are solely the responsibility of the authors and do not reflect policy or program interests of the Ford Foundation.

2.

The SAT Score Decline:
Facts, Figures and Emotions

William U. Harris

The November 10, 1975 issue of the *U.S. News and World Report* summarized a study that was done for the U.S. Office of Education by the University of Texas at Austin. The study indicated that "... about one fifth of the adult population (in America)—23 million Americans—is found to have difficulty coping with everyday chores such as shopping, getting a driver's license or reading an insurance policy." Extensive testing revealed such things as:

1. Adults not able to figure the correct change from a $20 bill if given a drugstore receipt itemizing and adding up purchases—(28 percent could not).
2. Persons not able to fill out a bank check correctly—(14 percent could not).
3. Persons not knowing that the normal body temperature is 98.6 degrees Fahrenheit—(27 percent did not know).

The study further revealed that in the area of reading, 21.7 percent were found functionally incompetent, and another 32.2 percent were placed in the category labeled "Just Gets By."

William U. Harris is Area Director for the College Board Admissions and Guidance Programs at Educational Testing Service, Princeton, New Jersey. The author wishes to thank his colleagues at ETS and the College Board for granting him permission to summarize their thinking and writing in the preparation of this article.

Similar dismal percentages were found for the areas of problem-solving, computation and writing.

Although questions can be asked about the research design and methodology, and the population sampled, this is a sad commentary on the literacy problem in the world's best educated nation. When one considers this commentary in the context of the SAT score decline, it is no wonder that the issue has elicited highly charged emotions on the part of students, parents, schools, colleges, communities, politicians, and the like.

I suppose there are psychological, educational, social and other benefits to be derived from emotionalizing about a problem of this magnitude. However, excessive emotionalism, as manifested through the finger-pointing syndrome, or the citation of blame exercise, becomes dysfunctional, and will probably add little to empirical efforts designed to explain the causes, and offer alternative solutions. I seek in this article to summarize the known facts and figures about the phenomenon. I do so with the realization that what's fact to one might be fiction to another. But, I realize, as did Aldous Huxley, that: "Facts do not cease to exist because they are ignored." Just as relevant is Mark Twain's suggestion: "First get your facts; and then you can distort them at your leisure."

Let's begin with the fact that SAT score averages have declined for 12 years, since 1963. The verbal scores have declined 41 points from the testing year 1962-63 to the testing year 1974-75. During the same period the math scores declined 29 points. During the 1974-75 testing year, the verbal and mathematical score declines for college-bound seniors were the largest for any single year since the decline was first observed. Regarding the way scores have distributed themselves, there has been a higher frequency of low scores attained, and a lower frequency of high scores. The verbal decline has been larger than the decline in mathematical scores.

The obvious sequel to these factual statements is the question: "Why are SAT score averages declining?" The most straightforward answer we can give is: "We do not know the reasons at this time." However, as Dr. Sidney P. Marland, Jr., President of the College Entrance Examination Board, stated at the Annual Business Meeting of the Board in October, 1975, ". . . we take seriously our responsibility to try to explain the phenomenon as dependable evidence is assembled." To attest to this proclamation, the College Board, working cooperatively with ETS, has established a Blue Ribbon advisory panel headed by Willard Wirtz, former Secretary of Labor and now President of the National Manpower Institute, to assess various theories for the decline. The panel, which is comprised of some of the nation's top measurement experts, social scientists and other scholars and citizens, has already begun to meet. During its two-year life span, the panel will give primary emphases to examining the SAT itself, and the changing populations of students taking the test. The panel will have a plethora of hypotheses with which to concern itself.

Hypotheses for the decline can be generally listed under four headings: *changes in society, changes in the schools, changes in the testing population,* and *problems with the tests.* It is when looking within these categories that one learns and understands the specific explanations that various publics are offering for the score decline.

Hypotheses
Changes in Society
None of the institutions in our society has escaped accusing fingers for the decline. An editorial in the November 9, 1975 issue of the *Washington Post* entitled "The Great SAT Mystery," stated:

> The decline in college entrance test scores throughout the country offers an irresistible opportunity to all the philosophers of American culture. Since nobody really knows why the scores are dropping, you can pick up whichever explanation you like best with the assurance that it's as defensible as any other. You won't often get a chance like this one."

If you haven't already picked an explanation, you might get some ideas from these:

1. Regarding the *family*—it has become too permissive, parents have abdicated their authoritative role; parents are too indulgent, too coddling; the Women's Liberation movement has had an effect on a large number of women who are full-time mothers; the divorce rate is higher; there have been changes in expectations for education.

2. Regarding *religion*—there has been a growing rejection of traditional Western religions and a concomitant search for meaning and relevance in other areas, i.e., religions of the East, drug-related religions, witchcraft, astrology.

3. Regarding *civil rights*—we are seeing increased encroachment of the courts, as evidenced by busing and other efforts which have caused an upheaval in school programs and attendance; increased legislative involvement in education, having the effect sometimes of seeming to tie the hands of school personnel on matters such as discipline; and greater access to higher education.

4. Regarding *crisis of values*—we are experiencing a revolution in values, including a decline in the Protestant ethic, specifically the obsolescence of the idea of success through hard work; the impact of the counter-culture with its hostility to reason, to science, to technology, to industry, to the work ethic; subversive political activity of Communists; and organized crime's efforts in promoting pornography.

There are other societal changes in national priorities, in the economy, and changes due to technological advancements and the labor movement in education that are hypothesized to have had an effect on scores.

Although the explanations under societal changes are sensitive, they seem to elicit less emotionalism than do those offered under the heading, *Changes in the Schools*. This is understandable, since we who work in the area of education frequently tend to become defensive about our livelihood.

Changes in the Schools

How often have you heard, or been asked to defend, the following speculations that were offered without supporting documentation?

1. Various school curricula have increasingly deemphasized aural-oral communication skills, reading and writing skills and modern foreign language study. The decline can be attributed to the emergence of "new math"; to open schools; to the effects of reading programs without emphasis on phonetics, vowels, etc.; to the adaptation of the pass/fail system and the deemphasis on grades; to the stress on independent study; and to different curricula followed by different ethnic groups.

2. Some say that institutional policies, such as automatic promotion of students regardless of course mastery, less homework and failure to group students by ability, have either singularly or multiply caused the decline.

3. Die-hard critics of schools would never let the teachers escape when offering self-styled explanations about the score decline. They feel there has been too much influence by the "soft pedagogical left" who believe "expressiveness is an adequate substitute for thinking and knowing" and who view leniency as a kindness to the underprivileged. They suggest that the influx into the profession of greater numbers of married females who are distracted and less dedicated, and the invasion of male teachers and principals in the 1960s into the traditionally female domain, have created an ill-prepared student population. The explanations go on: for example, too many inexperienced teachers are hired in grades K-6; there is too much reliance on clerical and instructional aides by teachers; the poorly educated teacher projects his/her own low level of academic achievement onto the students; and, there is too much hesitancy to enforce academic standards, to discipline students and to rid students of the fantasy that everyone has won, and all must have prizes.

4. As for students, there are negative attitudes toward education, a decline in competitiveness, and truancy, alcohol and drugs.

Changes in the Testing Population

As the previously mentioned *Washington Post* editorial suggested, the next category, *Changes in the Testing Population*, will be the choice of seers who take their inspiration from the history of the Roman Empire. They will welcome this bit of evidence of the incipient decay around us. They offer in evidence arguments that today's degenerate population has fewer able students going directly to college; that fewer students repeat grades because of poor performance, and even those who do are less able than their counterparts of past years; that there are more educationally disadvantaged; that larger numbers of very able females have migrated to the technologies; and that the post-World War II baby population is unusual in character when one considers family size, structure and socioeconomic status (SES).

Problems with the Test

Lastly, there are those who advocate that the real problem is not with the population, or the schools, or with society, but with the test itself, which is improperly scaled and/or equated; that the test lacks "linguistic clarity," or is irrelevant and culturally biased.

The hypotheses go on and on. But what are the empirical data that have been gathered to substantiate each? What are the *facts* as we know them? Since the hypotheses could be broadly categorized under the four headings of *changes in society, problems with the tests, changes in the testing population* and *changes in the schools*, it seems reasonable to look at research as it relates to those same categories.

Research

Changes in Society

When one examines scattered research related to the score decline, there is evidence to indicate that there may have been subtle factors operating in the society, especially in the post-World War II baby boom population. The well-known negative correlation between family size and test performance (children from larger families tend to score lower, on the average, than children from smaller families on almost all kinds of mental tests) is such a factor. Since family size was increasing during the period of the post-World War II population surge, the relationships between family size and test scores would predict a decline in the scores for the high school cohort beginning in about 1963, precisely when the SAT decline did, in fact, begin.

Zajonc (1975) has shown how mean birth rank, another changing characteristic of the 1946-1956 birth years, correlates with the SAT and other score declines. It has been pointed out by others that the population increase was disproportionate by SES groups, with high-and middle-SESs contributing more to the boom than did low-SES families. But an increase in the higher-SES part of the population in the late 1940s would have tended to produce higher rather than lower scores in the mid-1960s because of the correlation of SES and test performance. With such an assortment of possible influences operating, it would be surprising if average scores on tests like the SAT had remained stable during the period of the declines. Change would be anticipated. But the direction of change would be difficult to predict.

As has been suggested by many persons, undoubtedly the rise of television during the same period also has had some impact. However, just what that impact has been is not clear. Roger Farr, a reading expert from Indiana University, has argued that television may enhance reading ability. In a review of reading abilities at several population levels by Farr, it was suggested that reading ability in both public and private schools increased from the 1930s until about 1965. Even though a slight decline in reading ability was observed since 1965, students still read better than did students in 1945.

Yet another view of trends in the population was observed with the renorming of the Stanford Binet test in 1970. The Stanford Binet test, originally normed in 1937, showed a gain in the ability of the national population when the test was renormed.

Problems with the Tests

The psychometric quality of the SAT is, and has always been, under scrutiny by ETS, working on behalf of the College Board. Internally, techniques are and have been routinely used to ensure that various forms of the SATs are comparable in difficulty, from administration to administration, and from year to year. The efforts of our research convince us that the score decline is not evidence of some technical factor in constructing, scoring or calibrating the tests prior to reporting the scores.

Externally, surveys are done of colleges who use the free Validity Study Service to determine the predictive power of the SAT for them. A recent survey of a sample of colleges which had conducted at least four comparable validity studies during the first 10 years of the decline revealed no indication of a change in the validity of the SAT. The test was found to be just as predictive of academic performance in college as it had been in the past.

Concerning the relevance of the SAT to school curricula, we must continue to emphasize that the test was not designed nor intended to measure school performance. The SAT was designed to measure long-term developed verbal and mathematical reasoning abilities, attributes that are related to college performance.

Changes in the Testing Population

Since some hypothesize that there has been a change in the population of students taking the test, logical, researchable questions would appear to be: What is the nature of the change that has occurred? How much of the change can be attributed to the change in the mix of colleges requiring the SAT? Or, how much is due to the number of times a student repeats the test? How much gain can be expected when tests are repeated? How has the influx of women and ethnic minorities affected the SAT scores?

In 1960 and 1966 ETS conducted for the College Board norm studies for a test similar to the SAT that is usually taken by high school juniors, the Preliminary Scholastic Aptitude Test. A third norming study of this test (now called the Preliminary Scholastic Aptitude Test/National Merit Scholarship Qualifying Test) was done in 1974 by researchers at ETS. There was virtually no change in the mean scores obtained by the national samples of high school juniors from 1960 to 1974.

Flanagan and Jung of the American Institutes for Research, in the Project TALENT Study, investigated possible changes in reading comprehension covering the period from 1960 to 1970. The study, which involved over 400,000 high school students from a random sample of 1353 different schools, revealed a slight increase in reading test performance during the 10-year period.

The preliminary findings of a study begun in 1975 by ETS, which focused on the number of score reports sent to certain colleges by the CEEB candidate population, suggest noticeable changes in the patterns of score reporting for the academic years 1960-61, 1966-67 and 1973-74. For example, from 1960-61 to 1973-74, the proportion of SAT score reports going to the most selective liberal arts colleges decreased from 13.2 percent to 5.6 percent. According to results, College Board candidates have changed substantially in their patterns of college applications during the period studied. However, the extent, if any, to which the changes have contributed to the score decline cannot be determined by this study.

At least two kinds of score decline explanations have surfaced relating to repetition of the SAT. First, recent years have seen a smaller proportion of students taking the SAT as juniors and repeating it as seniors. This steady decline has been evident since about 1962. Since this repeating pattern overlaps the period of the score decline, it is attractive as a possible explanation. Nevertheless, both Marco and Stern (1975) and McCandless (1975), after analyses of this hypothesis, concluded that no more than about three points of the score decline could be accounted for in this way.

A second-repeater hypothesis suggests that those who repeat the test today experience smaller gains in their scores than those who repeated several years ago. During the spring of 1974, a study was undertaken to investigate the extent to which decreasing numbers of repeaters from junior-year to senior-year might help account for the score decline. Previous studies showed that seniors who repeat the test have higher scores, and that junior-to-senior-year repetition resulted in an average increase of about 15 points. The study showed that repeaters did have an effect but that they were not a perceptible cause of the decline.

But can't one conclude that the change in repeater patterns and other indicators reflects a change in students' attitudes toward the SAT? It is conceivable that a change in attitude would follow from the situation of recent years which found colleges actively recruiting students rather than selecting them from large applicant pools. Such an attitudinal explanation is one that could explain the reductions in SAT scores at the higher levels. For example, the absolute number of students scoring in the very high ranges of SAT scores has declined. In 1967, more than 30,000 persons scored in the 700-800 range on the verbal portion of the SAT; this absolute number of scores in the 700-800 range declined gradually until, in 1975, it was only about 15,000. This gradual decrease in scores in the high ranges has occurred despite fluctuations in the total numbers of students taking the SAT. How much the attitudes of SAT test-takers affect this, we are not sure.

When making reference to changes in the test-taking population, it is often hypothesized that the increase in minorities and women are negatively correlated with the decline of the SAT scores. Have scores declined because larger numbers of women take the SAT? No! Although a larger proportion of women now take the SAT, that proportion has increased very slowly—less than one percent a year. It is doubtful that an increase of that nature has caused the score decline. Besides, there is no appreciable difference between the performance of men and women on the verbal portion of the SAT; and SAT-verbal shows a sharper decline than SAT-mathematical. Also, score averages have declined for men as well as for women.

As for minorities, it is an established fact that minority college enrollments have increased and that, on the average, minorities tend to score lower on a test like the SAT. It is interesting, therefore, to examine the possibility that increased minority enrollments have contributed to the decline in the SAT test score averages. According to data available, 10.8 percent of the freshman class in public four-year colleges in the fall of 1966 were either black or American Indian. By 1972, this figure had increased to 15.9 percent. The increases in minority enrollments were not limited to public institutions. In 1966, 2.4 percent of students in private universities were black or American Indian. In 1972, this figure was 5.4 percent. With such a small increase in the proportion of the total college enrollment, however, it is unlikely that a large part of the SAT score decline could be attributed to this source. Moreover, there has not been a significant increase in the proportion of minorities taking the SAT during the years 1971-72, 1972-73, 1973-74, 1974-75, yet the SAT averages continue to decline, and they saw the biggest single-year decline to date in 1974-75.

More important than increases in minority enrollments could be increases in enrollment of low-SES students. Research done in the years 1957 to 1967 indicates that the proportion of low-SES students attending two-year and four-year colleges has been increasing more rapidly than the proportion of high-SES students. Since the correlations between SES and test scores is well known, the shifts in college-going patterns by SES groups present some explanation for that part of the decline which occurred between 1963 and 1967. However, since about 1971, there has been a decrease in proportions of cohorts entering college. Unless there was a concomitant decrease in high- and middle-SES students going on to college, a proportional increase in low-SES students during this later period would not be possible for immediate college entrants.

Currently, additional research is being pursued on two fronts—research into stability of the SAT verbal score scale and into the question whether the decline in scores for SAT candidates can be attributed to systematic changes in the composition of the groups sitting for the test.

Changes in the Schools

As previously mentioned, the most popular explanation for the SAT score decline is that students now graduating from American high schools are less capable than those in previous years. The primary focus of this explanation has been the quality of instruction in the schools. No better rebuttal can be made to this explanation than the one emphasized by Dr. Marland in his remarks to the previously referenced Annual Business Meeting of the Board. He remarked:

". . . It might be useful to consider what the SAT is and what it does. *First*, let me suggest what the SAT is *not*. It was not designed as a measure of school performance and should not be used for that purpose. To single out the schools as being responsible for the decline is unwarranted, unfair and scientifically unfounded.

"*Secondly*, the SAT is *not* a measure of some innate and unchanging quality that somehow mystically categorizes people. It does not gauge the worth of a human being, or his or her capacity to function well or creatively in society.

"What, then, *is* the SAT? It is a measure of developed verbal and mathematical reasoning abilities. It measures those abilities that are most commonly needed for academic performance in colleges and universities. . . It is intended to supplement the school record and other information about the student in assessing competence to do college work.

"It is a uniform measure of the same mental tasks, expressed on a common scale for all students. Thus it operates as a "leveling agent," or, if you will, a democratizing agent, cutting across differences in local customs and conditions, and affording admissions officers a uniform measure that, taken together with other data, helps in the assessment of the *academic* potential of students in relation to the differing academic demands of institutions.

"The SAT is both supplemental and incremental, and can effectively improve the prediction of college grades when combined with high school records and achievement test scores. Thousands of colleges, public and private, large and small, have proven this to their own satisfaction, and continue to today. Therefore, let me emphasize that the SAT still does what it was designed to do just as well as ever—probably better, for reasons of constant validation over the years. The predictive validity of the SAT in helping forecast college performance remains as strong and as high as it has been in past decades; the decline in scores has not affected this function of the test, and I want to stress that fact."

Conclusion

You can surmise from the preceding that based on research evidence now available, no firm conclusions can be drawn about the reason(s) for the score decline. You can also surmise that it will be difficult, if not impossible, to amass data to confirm or reject all of the hypotheses. In spite of the inconclusiveness, the phenomenon does have some implications for colleges and universities, secondary schools and the students themselves.

For colleges and universities, I would suggest that SAT scores are still constant and reliable measures, and they continue to predict student performance in college. Collegiate administrative officers and admissions people may consider adjusting their sights to the way their incoming students distribute themselves over the SAT score scale, and avail themselves of the Board's free Validity Study Service. The use of this service will enhance the institutions' knowledge about scores they receive and about score interpretation as it relates to their particular situation.

For secondary schools that are obviously uneasy about this information, realize that the SAT was not designed to be a measure of the quality of education of the high schools. It was designed to measure the kinds of abilities that generally develop very slowly over the student's entire academic life. These abilities are heavily dependent on learning experiences outside the classroom as well as on learning experiences within the classroom. Those schools that are being charged with responsibility for the score decline are being charged inappropriately. There may be a degree of responsibility yet to be discovered, but at present there is no basis for saying that the SAT score decline is attributable to the schools themselves.

For students who are going on to college, realize that the score decline does not necessarily mean that they will not be able to get into college. On the contrary, circumstances are such that it is more likely that young people will have greater opportunity for college and university admission in the future. The population pool of 17- to 18-year-olds will be diminishing within the next decade, and colleges and universities will likely adjust their programs to reflect sensitivity to the anticipated divergence.

References and Suggested Readings

American Council on Education. *The American Freshman: National Norms for Fall, 1972.* ACE Research Reports, Volume 7, No. 5, 1972.

Angoff, W.H. Why the SAT Scores Are Going Down. *The English Journal,* March 1975, 10-11.

Breland, H.M. *The SAT Score Decline: A Summary of Related Research.* Princeton, New Jersey: Educational Testing Service, January 1976.

College Entrance Examination Board. *College-Bound Seniors, 1974-75.* New York: College Entrance Examination Board, 1975.

Jackson, R. *A Summary of SAT Score Statistics for College Board Candidates.* Princeton, New Jersey: Educational Testing Service, December 1975.

Marco, C.C. and J. Stern. *The Stability of the SAT Score Scale (ETS RB-75-9).* Princeton, New Jersey: Educational Testing Service, April 1975.

Marland, S.P., Jr. SAT Score Decline. A reprint from remarks delivered at the Annual Business Meeting of the College Entrance Examination Board, October 1975.

McCandless, S.A. The SAT Score Decline and Its Implications for College Admissions. A paper presented at the 1975 Western Regional Meeting of the College Entrance Examination Board, January 1975.

The Washington Post. The Great SAT Mystery, November 9, 1975.

U.S. News and World Report. Modern Life Is Too Much for 23 Million Americans, November 10, 1975, 84.

Zajonc, R.B. Intellectual Environment and Intellectual Development: New Data and New Implications. Invited paper prepared for the Annual Meeting of the Midwestern Psychological Association, Chicago, Illinois, May 2, 1975.

3.

The Decline in ACT Test Scores: What Does It Mean?

Richard L. Ferguson

Very few phenomena in recent years have captured the interest of the press, educators and the public with a fervor equal to that accorded the now well documented decline in students' scores on achievement and aptitude tests. Major stimulants of that interest have been the reports of declines in college entrance examination scores on both the ACT Assessment Program of the American College Testing Program (Ferguson and Maxey, 1976; Munday, 1976) and the Scholastic Aptitude Test of the College Entrance Examination Board (Angoff, 1975; McCandless, 1975; Scully, 1975). Nor have the reports of test score declines been limited strictly to college entrance examinations or to college students. Harnischfeger and Wiley (1975) have assembled data based on a wide variety of testing programs and concluded that test scores have been declining for about a decade in all grades from five upwards.

Much of the discussion about the decline has focused on speculation about its causes. For some critics of our educational systems, declining test scores represent a confirmation of their worst fears about schools—that the schools are failing in their primary task of educating children. These critics attribute the

Richard L. Ferguson is Vice President, Research and Development Division, The American College Testing Program, Iowa City, Iowa.

decline to such factors as excessive permissiveness in the schools, lowered expectations for students and less concern by school faculty with the teaching of the "basic" skills. Many educators, on the other hand, have taken a defensive posture by blaming factors external to the school, such as parents, television and various social forces, as the principal causes of the decline.

For the most part, none of these possible causes for the decline is either entirely substantiated or refuted by existing data. In considering reasons for the decline, it is important to note that very vew data have been collected in the past 10 years which would permit conclusive generalizations about the causes of the decline. Because the collection of such data was not a priority at the inception of the decline in the mid-1960s and because such data are expensive to collect and analyze, no systematic collection procedures have been employed to assemble a data base adequate for permitting *definitive* statements about the decline we are experiencing today. At best, existing data permit us to (1) describe the characteristics of the decline for specific testing programs, and (2) begin to evaluate some preliminary hypotheses about its causes. It is the purpose of this article to do both of these things, and to briefly consider possible implications of the decline for education.

To shed as much light on the declining test score phenomenon as possible, pertinent ACT data are presented here in a succinct question-and-answer format. More detailed discussions of the important points are available in research reports currently available at ACT (Ferguson and Maxey, 1976; Maxey, Wimpey, Ferguson and Hanson, 1976; Munday, 1976).

Nature and Extent of the
ACT Test Score Decline

By way of background, the ACT is a guidance-oriented assessment program completed each year by approximately one million college-bound students. The assessment battery includes an Interest Inventory, a Student Profile Section which collects about

200 pieces of background information on students, and four academic subtests, one each in English, mathematics, social studies and natural sciences. A brief content outline of each of the ACT subtests is included in Table 1. The data reviewed in this article relate primarily to student scores on the four subtests and to the ACT Composite Score, which is computed as the arithmetic average of the four subtest scores. The ACT score scale ranges from a low score of 1 to a maximum score of 36.

How Large Is the Decline in ACT Test Scores?

As the data in Figure 1 indicate, over the past 11 years for which ACT data are available (1964-65 through 1974-75), the average ACT Composite Score for college-bound students has declined about 1.6 standard scores, or about one-third of a standard deviation. In 1964-65, the mean ACT Composite Score was 19.9; by 1974-75 it had dropped to about 18.3. This represents an average decline of approximately three percent of a standard deviation over each of the past 11 years. The magnitude of the ACT score decline is highly comparable to the magnitude of the decline experienced for the SAT (McCandless, 1975).

Is the Decline Significant?

As Munday (1976) observes in a recent ACT Research Report, a decline of three percent of a standard deviation in any given year is small and probably of no great significance, since it might easily be attributed to chance. However, an *average* decline of three percent over an 11-year period *is* significant, and suggests that factors other than chance were almost certainly at work to bring it about.

Is the Decline Apparent Across All Content Areas?

Data reported by Ferguson and Maxey (1976) indicate that the magnitude of the decline in ACT test scores is not consistent

Table 1

Content Outline of the ACT Subtests

ENGLISH USAGE TEST—This test is a 75-item, 40-minute test that measures the student's understanding and use of the basic elements in correct and effective writing: punctuation, grammar, sentence structure, diction, style, logic and organization. The test gives considerably greater weight to the analysis of clear and effective expression than to rote recall of rules of grammar. The test consists of several prose passages with certain portions underlined and numbered. For each underlined portion, four alternative responses are given. The student must decide which alternative is correct or most appropriate in the context of the passage.

MATHEMATICS USAGE TEST—This test is a 40-item, 50-minute examination that measures the student's mathematical reasoning ability. It emphasizes the solution of practical quantitative problems which are encountered in many college curricula and includes a sampling of mathematical techniques covered in high school courses. The test emphasizes reasoning in a quantitative context, rather than memorization of formulas, knowledge of techniques or computational skill. The format of the item is a question with five alternative answers, the last of which may be "none of the above."

SOCIAL STUDIES TEST—This test is a 52-item, 35-minute test that measures the analytical and evaluative reasoning and problem-solving skills required in the social sciences. There are two general types of items: the first type is based on reading passages, the second on general background or information obtained primarily in high school social studies courses. All items are multiple choice with four alternatives. The items based on the reading passages require not only reading comprehension skills, but also the ability to draw inferences and conclusions, to extend the thoughts of the passage to new situations, to make deductions from experimental or graphic data, and to recognize a writer's bias, style and mode of reasoning.

NATURAL SCIENCES TEST—This test is a 52-item, 35-minute test that measures the critical reasoning and problem-solving skills required in the natural sciences. There are two general types of items: the first is based on reading passages, the second on information about science. All items are multiple choice with four alternatives. The passages concern a variety of scientific topics and problems; descriptions of scientific experiments and summaries of procedures and outcomes of experiments are the most common formats. The items require the students to interpret, analyze, synthesize and evaluate the concepts and ideas in the passages, and in particular to understand the purpose of experiments, the logical relations between experimental hypotheses and the generalizations which can be drawn from the experiments.

47

Figure 1

*ACT Mean Composite Scores: 1964-65 Through 1974-75
for College-Bound Students*

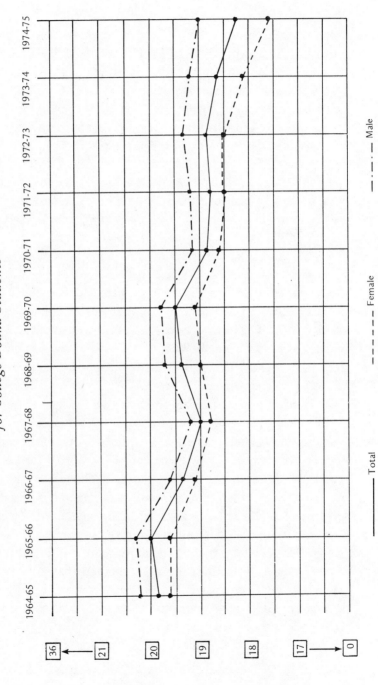

across all content areas. Social studies showed the greatest decline
in test scores; in 1964-65 the mean score for the Social Studies
Test was 20.6 as opposed to 17.1 in 1974-75. This represents an
over-all decline of approximately three-and-one-half standard
scores. Mathematics scores declined from 19.6 to 17.4, or about
two standard scores during the same time period. A drop from
18.7 to 17.3, representing a decline of approximately one-and-
one-half standard scores, has occurred in English. The only
content area for which test scores did not decline was natural
sciences. For that discipline, mean scores actually increased, from
20.4 to 20.8, a gain of about one-half of a standard score over the
11-year period.

Is the Decline Comparable
for Both Sexes?

The ACT data in Figure 1 indicate substantial differences in
the magnitude of the decline for men and women. Over-all, the
average ACT Composite Score has dropped about 1.2 standard
scores for men (from 20.2 to 19.0) since 1964-65; at the same
time, the average Composite Score dropped about 2.1 standard
scores for women (from 19.7 to 17.6).

With the exception of mathematics, in every area where a
decline has occurred, ACT test scores have dropped more for
women than for men. Specifically, the scores indicate a decline in
mathematics scores for women from 18.0 to 16.1, or 1.9 standard
scores. While mathematics test scores declined slightly more for
men than for women, the men still maintained higher average test
scores in mathematics. English test scores declined for men from
17.7 to 16.6, or 1.1 standard scores; for women they declined
from 19.9 to 18.0, or 1.9 standard scores. Thus, although test
scores in English declined more for women than for men, on the
average women continued to score higher on the English test. The
decline in ACT test scores is most pronounced in the social
studies. There, men's test scores have declined by 2.3 standard
scores, 20.6 to 18.3, since 1964-65. At the same time, women's

scores declined from 20.6 to 16.1, a drop of 4.5 standard scores.

The only content area resisting a decline in test scores was the natural sciences. The mean scores for natural sciences remained approximately stable for women at 19.7 and actually increased by 1 standard score, 21.0 to 22.0, for men.

Is the Decline Observable in All States and All Geographic Regions

Using ACT data based on those states having sizable and relatively stable numbers of students taking the ACT tests in each of the last five years, Munday (1976) has determined that the declines in ACT test scores have occurred in nearly all states and regions of the country in which the ACT is heavily used. With the exception of eastern states, where the SAT is the test predominantly used, ACT data include states in all parts of the country. In general, these data indicate that the decline in scores is less marked in the Western states than in the Southern and North Central states. Except for two states in the North Central region, all states show a decline. Since data from the College Entrance Examination Board show a decline in SAT scores in the Eastern states, there is no doubt but that the decline in college entrance test scores has occurred in all regions of the country.

Has There Been a Decrease in the Number of High Scoring Students?

Maxey *et al.* (1976) report that when a randomly selected sample of ACT test score data collected over the last five years (1970-71 through 1974-75) are assigned to four score intervals— 1-15, 16-20, 21-25 and 26-36—several interesting outcomes are observed. First, the percentage of high scoring students (i.e., those scoring in the 26-36 interval) has been highly stable each year, at about 14 percent. The percentage of low scoring students (i.e., those scoring in the 1-15 interval), however, has increased from about 27 percent to 33 percent. This finding is consistent across all of the content areas except natural sciences, which remained relatively stable at both ends of the distribution. The greatest increase in percentage of low scores occurred in social studies, which increased from 32 percent to 44 percent. In summary, the percentage of students scoring high on the ACT subtests has remained about the same over the past five years, whereas the percentage of low scoring students has increased each year. This is in direct contrast to SAT data (Harnishfeger and Wiley, 1975; Scully, 1975) which appear to indicate a decrease in the percentage of high scoring students on the SAT over about the same period of time. Like the ACT data, however, SAT data show an increase in the percentage of low scoring students.

Is the Increase in the Number of
Low-Scoring Students Comparable
for Both Sexes?

ACT data clearly indicate that the percentage increase of students scoring at the lower intervals on the ACT tests was much more dramatic for women than for men. Specifically, the percentages of high and low scoring men have remained essentially constant over the past five years, whereas the percentage of women in the high scoring interval declined from 12 percent to 10 percent. At the same time, the percentage of low scoring women increased from 28 percent to 37 percent. This finding must be tempered by the fact that the percent of the total ACT-tested population represented by women has increased from 49 percent to 53 percent over the past five years. It is likely, therefore, that the pool of college-bound women has increased substantially and now necessarily includes more women with less well developed academic ability than in the past.

Summary of ACT Data
Describing the Decline

In summary, the ACT (and SAT) data indicate a steady decline in test score averages over the past decade. The extent of the decline has been similar for both programs. In any given year the decline is small, but the cumulative decline is large, well-documented and cannot be attributed entirely to chance factors. There is variation in the decline in ACT test scores by subject matter field; the decline is largest in social studies, followed in order by English and mathematics. No decline, but rather a small increase, has occurred in the natural sciences. The decline has occurred in all regions and nearly all states of the country. The percentage of high scoring students has remained about the same in recent years, whereas the percentage of low scoring students has increased. Finally, there are marked sex differences in the decline, with men's mean Composite Scores declining by 1.2 standard scores in the past decade and women's by 2.1 standard scores. This phenomenon has occurred simultaneously with an increase in the number of ACT-tested college-bound women.

What Are the Causes of the
Test Score Decline?

Any discussion of the causes for the decline in ACT test scores must be approached with great caution. Although the data presented in this section may bear in a significant way on the reasons for the decline, no vehicle exists for establishing a causal relationship between the decline and the variables for which ACT data are reported. This fact speaks strongly against unwarranted and unqualified generalizations about causes for the decline in ACT scores. As in the previous section, *possible* explanations for the ACT test score decline are discussed in a question and answer format.

Has the Content of
the Tests Changed?

Perhaps one of the most obvious questions to ask when considering possible causes for the ACT test score decline is whether the content of the ACT subtests has changed. Behind this question is the implication that ACT test scores might be declining because the subtests may not be measuring the same knowledge and skills today (i.e., those listed in Table 1) that they measured 10 years ago. ACT is confident that this is not a significant factor in the decline. The changes in test content over the past five to 10 years have been minor and appear to be too small to account for any significant aspect of the decline.

A related question and one more frequently asked involves whether the ACT tests are still measuring important skills, that is, whether the curriculum has changed and the tests have not kept up with that change. Again, this appears to be a highly improbable explanation for the decline. ACT's test development procedures, which depend on hundreds of high school and college teachers all over the country to write the ACT test materials each year, would seem to work against such an explanation. It is important to acknowledge, however, that the ACT subtests do not attempt to measure all of the important skills taught by the school. It is possible that what the ACT tests measure represent a smaller portion of the total curriculum today than it did a decade ago. For example, the language usage skills emphasized in the ACT English Usage Test may not account for as many hours of curriculum instruction as was once the case. Regardless, the tests do continue to measure many of the important skills taught. Convincing evidence of this latter point is provided in the form of data indicating continued high correlations between ACT test scores and high school and college grades (Ferguson and Maxey, 1976; Munday, 1976).

Can the Decline Be Attributed to a Changing Pool of Students?

One explanation given for the declining test scores is that the pool of college-bound students taking the ACT tests has been changing. Although all of the data needed to address that hypothesis in a thorough way are not available, some information exists which describes certain changes in the attributes of the students who have taken the tests over the last few years.

First, the standard deviations of the ACT score distributions have increased during the 11-year period for which complete ACT data are available. These data signify greater heterogeneity among the students being tested. This trend, which was most pronounced in the mid to late 1960s, is observed across all content areas.

Second, the percentage of the ACT-tested population which is female has increased from 45 percent in 1964-65 to 53 percent in 1974-75. As noted earlier, the increase in the number of women in the testing pool has been accompanied by an increase in the percentage of women scoring in the lower score intervals on the test. This suggests that included among the larger number of college-bound women taking the ACT tests in recent years is a substantial number who are less well prepared academically than their counterparts of past years. It is important to underscore the fact that it cannot be inferred from these data that the academic abilities of women, in general, are on the decline.

Third, ACT data indicate that the percentage of ACT-tested students representing minority groups has remained essentially stable over the past five years. In 1970-71, students from minority racial-ethnic backgrounds comprised 11 percent of the ACT population. That percentage was precisely the same in 1974-75.

Finally, ACT data (Munday, 1976) indicate that there have been only slight changes in the family incomes of ACT-tested students over the last five years. However, the sizable inflation which has occurred over that same time span suggests a significant decrease in the spending power of the families of ACT-tested students.

Taken collectively, all of these data show that there have been some changes in the backgrounds of the ACT-tested population. Although it is likely that these changes—greater heterogeneity, more low scoring women, more students from families with restricted incomes—have affected the ACT scores, no data exist which permit definitive explanations of the nature or magnitude of that impact.

Are Today's ACT-Tested Students
Weaker Academically Than Their
Counterparts in the Past?

ACT data provide no clear-cut evidence about whether the decline in ACT test scores can, in part, be attributed to less able or less well prepared students. Recognizing this fact, Munday (1976) collected test data from statewide assessment programs in Iowa and Minnesota. These data, which yielded findings consonant with those evidenced by the ACT data, and which were based on the test scores of nearly all students in those state systems over a period of years, led Munday to conclude that there is cause to seriously consider lower developed academic abilities as at least a partial reason for the decline.

From still another perspective, Harnischfeger and Wiley (1975) have documented some changes in the high school curriculum and in the course-taking behaviors of students which may offer some partial explanation of the decline. Specifically, they cite data which indicate a "considerable enrollment decline in academic courses" in recent years in the nation's schools. To the extent that the ACT Assessment and other tests tend to emphasize the knowledge and skills taught in such academic courses, the change in enrollment patterns could explain, in part, the observed trends in ACT test scores.

Summary

Certainly not all of the possible reasons for the decline in ACT test scores have been mentioned in this section. However, several very plausible hypotheses have been touched upon briefly. Given the complexity of the phenomenon, it seems likely that many factors have contributed in varying degrees to the decline in scores. It is doubtful whether further analysis of existing data bases will shed much additional light on the precise causes of the decline inasmuch as those data bases were not constructed for that purpose. If this is indeed the case, and if there is value to be derived from documenting major factors in the decline, then considerable resources will have to be devoted to collecting and interpreting additional data which yield more precise insights than data currently available.

Implications for Colleges of the Decline in ACT Test Scores

Another matter of considerable importance involves the implications of the decline in test scores for colleges. Significantly, most discussions of the test score decline appear to infer that the decline is a negative phenomenon. In general, most people associate the decline with some shortcoming either in our educational system or of the students in that system. This is an unfortunate interpretation of the data given our present inability to clearly identify the causes of the decline. Moreover, such interpretations are problematic because some of the hypothesized causes of the decline may be the result of responses by colleges to educational or social needs which are viewed to be at least as important as the development of students' over-all academic ability.

For example, one hypothesis suggested as a possible reason for the ACT test score decline involves the increase in the number of college-bound women who are ACT-tested. To the extent that society deems it desirable that college be an option open to larger numbers of women, it is reasonable to expect colleges to respond to that need by enrolling more women, even if many of those women have less well-developed abilities than their fellow students of five or 10 years ago.

This is not to say that standards of performance or requirements related to minimum entering competencies should be abandoned. Indeed, such prerequisites cannot reasonably be waived unless colleges are prepared to invest significant amounts of their resources in providing pre-college-level instruction to students who require it.

Another example of the potential inappropriateness of viewing the test score decline as a negative phenomenon involves the hypothesis that the decline is related to a de-emphasis by students and schools of the traditional academic courses. If, for example, fewer students are enrolling in academic courses today than in the past and if they are instead taking courses which emphasize other important skills and abilities not typically measured by the tests, then the schools and society might well argue that the net benefit to students, even if it means lowered proficiency in the traditional "academic-type" skills, is worth the price. It is more likely, of course, that society will demand both outcomes of its schools, and that it will fall to the schools to find ways of meeting that expectation.

Although the negative overtones associated with the test score decline may be misplaced or overemphasized, one fact is clear. As a group, today's college-bound students *are* scoring considerably lower on traditional measures than their counterparts of previous years. The corollary to this statement is that today's college-bound students are less well prepared in the knowledge and skills measured by the tests than college-bound students of five to 10 years ago.

Regardless of the causes of these trends, the net effect of the decline is that many colleges are faced with the problem of providing instruction to students with much more disparate academic backgrounds than in the past. Recognizing this fact, many colleges have implemented special programs to ease the transition from high school to college of students who are not adequately prepared academically. Other schools would like to take steps to address the problem but don't know where to begin.

Perhaps the most feasible approach for educators to take in dealing with the decline is to acknowledge that the decline is real, make deliberate efforts to determine the extent to which the skills measured in the tests are important to successful performance in their programs, and then to either deny admission to students who lack the prerequisite skills or to provide instructional programs designed to help ill-prepared students acquire the required skills. Clearly, the latter of these two approaches is likely to be the more acceptable to society. It seems probable that concerted efforts aimed at helping students who do not possess the skills necessary for success in college and, by inference, for success in their life work, would be of considerable merit regardless of the reasons of the test score decline.

References

Angoff, W.H. Why the SAT Scores Are Going Down. *English Journal*, March 1975.

Ferguson, R.L. and E.J. Maxey. *Trends in the Academic Performance of High School and College Students.* ACT Research Report No. 70. Iowa City, Iowa: The American College Testing Program, 1976.

Harnischfeger, A. and D.E. Wiley. *Achievement Test Score Decline: Do We Need to Worry?* Monograph of CEMREL, Inc., 1975.

Maxey, E.J., L.M. Wimpey, R.L. Ferguson and G.R. Hanson. *Trends in Selected Items of the ACT Assessment: 1970-71 to 1974-75.* Reseach Report No. 74. Iowa City, Iowa: The American College Testing Program, 1976.

McCandless, S.A. The SAT Score Decline and Its Implications for College Admissions. Paper presented at the 1975 Western Regional Meeting of the College Entrance Examination Board, January 1975.

Munday, L.A. *Declining Admissions Test Scores.* ACT Research Report No. 71. Iowa City, Iowa: The American College Testing Program, 1976.

Scully, M.G. Drop in Aptitude Test Scores Is Largest on Record. *Chronicle of Higher Education*, September 15, 1975.

4.

Assessing Educational Attainments

Roy H. Forbes

A portrait of American education is taking shape in the statistical sketchbook of the National Center for Education Statistics. The "artist" is the Center's Denver-based National Assessment of Educational Progress (NAEP).

This statistical information, collected on a continuing, nationwide basis, systematically measures the knowledge, skills and attitudes of groups of young Americans, as opposed to the traditional testing of individuals. It provides a picture of the status of American education through census-like surveys that cut across diverse strata of youths. Educational attainments are analyzed and reported to the public by age (9-, 13-, 17-year-olds and young adults 26 to 35), sex, race, geographic region, size and type of community and level of parental education.

NAEP, a project of the Education Commission of the States, has been assessing in 10 learning areas—art, career and occupational development, citizenship, literature, mathematics, music, reading, science, social studies and writing—since 1969. In two areas, science and writing, results of second assessments have been released; a second survey in reading achievement will be released in the fall of 1976 (see the Addendum to this volume, page 217).

Roy H. Forbes is Director, National Assessment of Educational Progress, Education Commission of the States, Denver, Colorado.

Through these re-assessments, comparisons are made with data collected in earlier assessments to establish trend-lines in educational achievement of different population groups in specific learning areas.

Considering the picture of American education as already traced by released National Assessment data, some areas call for improvement; others appear in a positive light.

Science Knowledge

Results from the second assessment in science appear discouraging. The data show that science knowledge among American students is declining. Between the first assessment in 1969-70 and the second in 1972-73, a national drop of two percentage points occurred.

Why the lag in scientific knowledge? One major theory for the cause of the drop in science knowledge is that during the Sputnik era science was of great interest to the nation. Now there is a widespread feeling that science and technology have done as much harm as good.

One encouraging point from NAEP's second assessment in science is that the percentage of rural students who could answer a typical science question increased at all three age levels, a trend that, if it continues, could bring rural students up to the national average by 1983.

Likewise, in a special study of regional trends, NAEP found that between the time of the two assessments, science achievement in the South—an area then undergoing major desegregation—did not decline as much as it did in the rest of the nation for either black or white students. In fact, the science knowledge of nine-year-old Southern blacks actually improved.

Writing Skills

In 1975 National Assessment also reported that "American teenagers are losing their ability to communicate through written English." Between the survey of writing skills taken first in 1970 and repeated in 1974, the project found that both 13- and 17-year-olds in 1974 used a simpler vocabulary, wrote in a shorter, "primer-like" style and with less coherency than their school counterparts four years earlier.

However, the writing skills of nine-year-olds improved in that four-year interval. Also, mastery of basic writing mechanics—such as punctuation, capitalization and word agreement—continued to be handled adequately by a great majority of youths at all three school-age levels. The "basics" in writing seem to be well in hand.

Why a decline in teenagers' writing abilities? Speculation points to our changed culture. Television has been targeted as a prime "culprit" in that youths could be losing the sense of written coherence through *visually* sensing what is coherent. Students are also assimilating the abbreviated, choppy language of advertising. Then there's the telephone: why write if you can just phone?

One thing to be considered by curriculum specialists, teachers and the public: students are writing differently. But are they writing more poorly? Society's changing attitudes just might indicate a need to rethink, to restructure, the Standard English form that is used as a writing model in most American schools.

Reading Ability

Again, on the plus side, National Assessment was asked by the National Right to Read Effort to conduct an assessment of functional literacy of 17-year-old students. Results of that 1974 survey, when compared with a similar NAEP reading assessment of the same age level in 1971, show that functional literacy of in-school 17-year-olds has improved by two percentage points.

More importantly, the data show that those who most needed to improve, did improve. For example: Students living in the inner-city areas scored 3.6 percentage points higher in 1974; youths in the extreme-rural communities gained 4.1 percentage points; and blacks gained 3.6 percentage points.

However, this particular assessment was only of the very basic reading skills essential for functioning in everyday life—reading road signs, maps, advertisements, forms and reference works. Several of the exercises merely required knowledge of the alphabetical organization of dictionaries and telephone books.

According to Right to Read's own definition of functional literacy, the NAEP statistics indicate that nearly 11 percent of 17-year-old students are still unable to perform such tasks as reading a newspaper or the labels on medicine bottles and foods. It is up to the general public to decide if it is content with the large disparities between basic reading levels of some groups of 17-year-olds.

Mathematics Skills

National Assessment has also detected problems in the abilities of certain young Americans to perform certain mathematics skills. The first survey, made during the 1972-73 school year, revealed that the majority of 17-year-olds and young adults have mastered the operations of addition, subtraction, multiplication and division when presented as computational exercises. But when it comes to applying these basic skills in everyday situations, these same young Americans founder.

It appears that many young consumers are not prepared to shop wisely because they cannot apply fundamental math principles to everyday buying decisions. For example, National Assessment found that less than one-half of the 17-year-olds and adults could successfully determine the most economical size of a product, that only 16 percent of the adults could balance a checkbook and that only 20 percent of the adults could correctly calculate a taxi fare.

Indeed, when it comes to mathematics, young Americans appear to be generally out of place in the marketplace. The survey suggests that the nation's youthful consumer has difficulty with any form of mental arithmetic. All age levels score low on the ability to estimate or approximate whether an answer is reasonable—a skill that is considered vital for consumer survival.

Sex Differences

National Assessment also found that there is a difference

between the sexes in consumer-mathematics skills. It is usually assumed that women do a major part of the buying, but males consistently outperform females on exercises involving buying and household situations.

These results raise some puzzling questions. If girls can read better than boys, as confirmed by NAEP assessments and other research data, and generally show higher skill-levels in computational math exercises, why can't females do better than males in working math "story" problems, especially in the everyday, household consumer-type math?

There are other striking disparities in the educational achievements of males and females that have surfaced in special analyses of National Assessment data. For example, NAEP's statistics show that males at all four age levels generally do better than females in four major subjects: mathematics, science, social studies and citizenship.

In the four other learning areas, females consistently outperform males to any large degree in only one (writing); maintain a slight advantage in one (music); and in the remaining two subjects (reading and literature) are above male achievement levels at age nine, then drop to lag behind males by the young adult ages, 26-35.

These findings are alarming as the public increasingly calls for an accounting from the schools for what is being *learned*, not just what is being *taught*. The NAEP data would seem to imply that females are being exposed to subtle, or perhaps not-so-subtle, forces—both within the education system and society in general—that discourage them from trying to achieve in certain areas. Although barriers based on sex are being lifted, and the visibility of women who are entering the traditional male professions has increased, it is becoming more and more important for society and the schools to encourage women to consider entering these fields.

Other Differences

Other disparities in educational attainment appear in National Assessment comparisons of achievements of youths living in a wide range of size and type of communities. Over seven years of assessment, the NAEP data unequivocally confirm that community-related inequalities in achievement do exist, because young Americans from the affluent suburbs generally perform far above youths from the inner cities in reading, writing, mathematics, science, social studies, citizenship and literature. Only in music does the trend reverse—and then just to the extent that inner-city and rural groups listen to TV musical programs far more frequently than the national average. When it comes to individual music performance, results reverse again and the affluent suburban youths are once more in the lead.

The idea that size and type of community can influence the quality—and equality—of the education of young people has spawned legal cases throughout the nation. The courts are being asked to determine whether or not disparities in the financing of school districts with diverse levels of wealth result in disparities of educational opportunity.

Determining if, and when, equal educational opportunity is achieved is a difficult goal. How can an equal educational opportunity be measured in the first place? National Assessment hopes to help provide some of the answers.

Conclusion

Education is a complex issue and sweeping generalizations about the over-all education system should not be made. Assessments provide vital resources useful in evaluating the output of our education system:

- information on what young people know and do not know about the subjects commonly taught in our schools;
- benchmarks against which it is possible to measure educational change and progress in the future; and
- sociological data necessary for comparisons of youngsters in the city and those in the suburbs, or blacks and

whites, or males and females, and other comparisons useful in serving the public.

But an assessment is only one instrument to be used by educators. Each educator must go beyond the results of any type of test or survey and determine needs, diagnose problems and prescribe alternative measures appropriate to each individual school system.

5.

Declining Test Scores:
Interpretations, Issues and
Relationship to Life-Based Education

Philip G. Kapfer, Miriam Bierbaum Kapfer
and Asahel D. Woodruff

Since the mid-1960s many achievement test scores have dropped. There is no need to recite the evidence here. Instead, we will provide some background in terms of the interpretations currently being offered for the declining scores. Based on the issues uncovered, we will then look at the relationship of standardized testing to life-based educational programs. Finally, we will deal with the problem of what is both appropriate and essential in public education programs in bicentennial America, and with the requirements of carefully matching evaluation designs to specific program designs.

Interpreting the Data

> "When *I* quote test data," Humpty Dumpty said in a rather scornful tone, "the scores mean just what I choose them to mean—neither more nor less."*

---

*Paraphrased from *Alice in Wonderland.*

Philip G. Kapfer is Research Professor, Department of Education, and Head, Learning Resource Center, Eccles Medical Sciences Library, University of Utah, Salt Lake City. **Miriam Bierbaum Kapfer** is Research Professor, Department of Special Education, and Co-Director, Life-Involvement Model, Bureau of Educational Research, University of Utah. **Asahel D. Woodruff** is Professor Emeritus, Department of Educational Psychology, University of Utah.

The following review of current opinion regarding test score slippage is intended to be representative rather than exhaustive. We have divided a substantial number of writers whose work has appeared during 1975 and 1976 into three large and sometimes overlapping groups. We will look at what the "educational ax grinders" (as we have termed them) on the left and on the right are saying. Then we will look at the position of the "data grinders" in the middle.

The Ax Grinders on the Left

The educational ax grinders on the left are basically opposed to the use of standardized testing data as a basis either for making important program decisions for schools or for making critical life decisions for students. Some writers in this group would throw out standardized tests altogether; others would restrict the extent of their use through sampling techniques; and most would place far less importance on the data obtained in cases where the use of such tests seemingly cannot be avoided. This group probably would include many advocates of the following kinds of educational approaches: open schools, learning centers, individualized instruction, humanistic education, values education, career education, affective education, and the like. These educators have never felt very comfortable with sole reliance on evaluative data from normed achievement tests, and have consistently tried to tailor alternative evaluation strategies to specific program goals.

Many spokespersons for this point of view can be found. In the July/August 1975 issue of *The National Elementary Principal*, devoted entirely to the issue of standardized testing in America, Kohn (1975) quoted MIT's well-known physicist, J.R. Zacharias, as follows:

> I feel emotionally toward the testing industry as I would toward any other merchants of death. I feel that way because of what they do to the kids. I'm not saying they murder every child—only 20 percent of them. Testing has distorted their ambitions, distorted their careers. Ninety-five percent of the American

population has taken an ability test. It's not something that should be put into the hands of commercial enterprises. I think the whole psychological test business should cease and desist. It's an outrage. Measurement is a very important thing to me. But it implies one-dimensionality. The mind is not one-dimensional (pp. 14-15).

Zacharias was characterized as being "passionately opposed to what he feels is a mindless, secretive, stagnant, technology-obsessed business that is hopelessly prone to all manner of abuses against the human spirit" (p. 15).

NEA Executive Director Terry Herndon (NEA, 1976) is also clearly against standardized tests. Herndon stated, "Standardized tests are like a lock on the mind, a guard at the factory gate" (p. 12). He justified the NEA demand for a moratorium on standardized testing on several bases, including the complexity of educational processes and human abilities, a lack of common agreement on educational goals in schools across the country, and possible damage to the creative potential of children.

Taking a somewhat more moderate view, Green (1975) suggested limiting the use of standardized testing data, while perhaps not eliminating such tests altogether. He stated,

... parents must not allow their children to be judged on the basis of aptitude and achievement test scores alone. They must insist that other factors be taken into consideration when planning a child's educational future. These factors include a child's interests and subjects which will challenge him intellectually and academically (p. 92).

Perrone (1975, 1976) suggested a number of useful alternatives to standardized testing, and summed up his view of the controversy in this way:

Do teachers, principals and parents want evaluation? Of course they do. But they increasingly want evaluation that addresses *their* educational concerns, takes cognizance of *their* intentions, supports children's personal and intellectual growth, and has some potential for improving the quality of particular classrooms and schools. The standardized testing generally conducted in schools today does not address these concerns to a high degree, if at all (1975, p. 97).

In *Today's Education*, Wilhelms (1975) dealt evenhandedly with test score declines in the past decade, after which he outlined the "trade-offs":

> If there has been a temporary falloff of computation skills in math, which we can easily remedy, are we to place no value at all on the great gains in mathematical insight and understanding? If student motivation has waned a bit in the sciences, should we not balance into the equation the enormous strides we are taking in the humanities? If we have to pay something in academic accomplishment—we don't, but suppose we did—for the beneficent effect of open education on human becoming, isn't the growth in personhood worth enormously more than anything we could lose (p. 48)?

That the emphasis in schools *should be and is* on more than just traditional knowledge and skills is a strongly held belief among many educators. In the lead editorial in the July/August 1975 issue of *The National Elementary Principal*, Houts (1975) stated:

> ... as a society we are beginning to work on a new series of assumptions: that the purpose of education is not to sort people but to educate them; that in a knowledge society, we need to expose as many people to education as possible, not to exclude them from it; that human beings are marvelously variegated in their talents and abilities, and it is the function of education to nurture them wisely and carefully; and not least, that education has an overriding responsibility to respect and draw upon cultural and racial diversity (p. 3).

This view of education as being more than just traditional learning is pervasive. In November, 1975, a conference involving 25 educational associations and government agencies was held in Washington, D.C., to consider the testing problem. Sponsored by the National Association of Elementary School Principals and the North Dakota Study Group on Evaluation, with funds from the Rockefeller Brothers Fund, conferees explored the educational, social and legal implications of the use of standardized achievement tests. One of the 25 groups represented at the meeting, the National Science Teachers Association (1976), reported the following as the first recommendation from the conference:

> The profession needs to place high priority on developing and disseminating new processes of assessment that more adequately consider the diverse talents, abilities and cultural backgrounds of children (p. 2).

A key idea in all of the above quotes can be expressed in the words "diverse talents." The degree of one's "leftness" on the ax grinding scale often can be gauged by the relative amount of concern expressed for developing such talents—that is, for talents other than the verbal skills and knowledge typically measured by standardized achievement tests.

The Ax Grinders on the Right

In contrast to the statements in the preceding section, the educational ax grinders on the right tend to interpret test score declines by urging us to get back to the "basics," to traditional methods and values, to sound discipline, to greater control of students in schools; and, thereafter, hopefully, to rising standardized test scores. Many such educators would eliminate "frills," "innovations" and "permissiveness." They would also tend to reduce program options and flexibility.

Representing this point of view is Max Rafferty (1976), ever willing and able to articulate the views of the far right. Should any reader's newspaper not carry Rafferty's column, here is a typical quote:

> Oh, sure. Since the tests show that the educators are doing a scurvy job, let's discredit the tests. There can't possibly be anything wrong with our "life adjustment" philosophy of peer-group acceptance, modular scheduling, non-graded pupil evaluation and, of course, "relevance." So let's just disregard anything that calls our whole professional way of thinking into question. It simply has to be wrong, because it's unthinkable that we should be (p. 5).

Assuming a more moderate position in *Today's Education*, Steven Muller (1975), President of The Johns Hopkins University, voiced the views of many concerned educators. Muller did not soft-pedal declining test scores. Rather, he pointed to an apparent loss of popular commitment to mass education as a reason for declining standards. He stated, ". . . costs are enormous, and there is growing concern that standards of achievement have suffered serious erosion. The questions of costs and standards intertwine" (p. 50). Muller then cited five factors related to declining test scores: (1) all people cannot be educated to the same level; (2) education for citizenship and education for economic productivity are not wholly congruent ideals; (3) mass education must deal with many unmotivated students; (4) the right of access to education and what is popularly referred to as a right "to education" are phrases having different meanings; and (5) the maintenance of high standards is dependent upon high quality (and expensive) instructors.

That Muller's appeal is definitely to the right is apparent from a congratulatory letter to him by Maehr (1976), published in a subsequent issue of *Today's Education*. Maehr, a junior high school teacher, stated, "We have schools without scholars, and those of us who object have been shouted down by the innovators, the faddists, the 'experts' long enough" (p. 8).

Obviously, Rafferty, Muller and Maehr are all to the right of center on our scale, but at somewhat different points. A common concern among all of them appears to be rather more the need to raise "educational standards" than to diversify programs to meet individual needs.

The Data Grinders in the Middle

The data grinders in the middle are the "true scholars" in any controversy, including the testing controversy, to the extent that they do not use the data to attempt to prove a predetermined point of view. Rather, they carefully qualify data interpretations and they suggest additional data-gathering focuses where needed. They point out fuzzy thinking and they admonish us to refrain from misusing results. It is probable that many, if not most, writers on the current testing controversy could at times be cited here—that they slip into and out of this category from time to time depending on what of their writing output one reads.

In particular, however, we would give high honors for data grinding to Harnischfeger and Wiley (1975) of CEMREL's ML-GROUP for Policy Studies in Education. During a four-month study, they re-ground old data, interrelated data from a variety of sources, drew both firm and tentative conclusions, outlined directional trends, and suggested a host of further studies that are needed in order to relate causes to effects. With Ford Foundation funding, their study resulted in a comprehensive report titled, *Achievement Test Score Decline: Do We Need to Worry?* (A summary of this report is available [1976] ; also, see their chapter in this present volume.) In brief, Harnischfeger and Wiley concluded that the decade-long decline in standardized test scores accurately indicates a genuine drop in student achievement. Among the possible causes postulated for the decline were the following: (1) decreasing enrollments in traditional, basic academic courses and in vocational training courses; (2) increases in elective or specialty courses; (3) lack of attention by test developers to new special courses; (4) dissimilarity of special courses from school to school; (5) shortened school days; and (6) circumscription of educationally important activities in the home because of extensive television viewing among older students. Harnischfeger and Wiley indicated no conclusive evidence in either direction regarding changes in students' learning motivation. They warned against over-reactions to test score declines that might result in untimely budgetary or program retrenchment.

Another well-supported effort at data grinding is the I/D/E/A (1975) publication, *The Decline in Achievement.* In an effort to isolate and analyze the causes for dropping test scores, I/D/E/A and The Thomas Alva Edison Foundation brought together leading educators, scientists and executives. Speculations of the conferees resulted in the compilation of a list of 20 factors that appear to be related to the drop in learning. These included television, work-study programs, less emphasis on basic fundamentals, leniency in grading, lack of motivation, lowered regard for achievement, broken homes, irrelevant teacher training programs, and increased student use of alcohol and drugs. The conferees concluded, "Changing values, changing content and general uncertainty have a profound influence upon student performance" (p. 19).

Another major organization obviously interested in the reasons for the declining national test scores is the College Entrance Examination Board. According to S.P. Marland, Jr. (1976), President of the CEEB, "To suggest curricular implications is not possible, for we do not know the reasons for the score decline. We have, however, appointed an external panel of measurement and other scholars to review the data . . ." (pp. 6-7). Presumably, the outcome of this study will provide additional indicators concerning causes for the score-drop problem.

Stake (1976) discussed the lower test scores as follows:

> . . . my guess is that the strongest force just now is that our teaching and learning do not stress "right answers" as they did earlier, though the tests still do. The students do not believe as much in "right answers" so they do not memorize them, or seek them, as they used to. An increasing number think the whole "right-wrong business" is a "put-on." If my guess is correct, some educators will rejoice to see their curricula succeeding in helping students to disdain simplistic answers; but others will be saddened by one more indicant of disrespect for ordinary teaching (pp. 6-7).

Stake then concluded with the following insightful comment: "If we continue to presume that these test scores do indicate quality of education, we will continue to be embarrassed for a long while" (pp. 6-7).

Possibly one of the more interesting explanations for declining test scores was presented by Tavris (1976). She reported extensively on the theory and research of R.B. Zajonc on the effects of birth order and family size on intelligence. According to Tavris, "Zajonc predicts that there will be a rise in SATs by 1980, give or take two years . . ." (p. 69). Zajonc determines the intellectual environment of a child by finding the mean of the absolute mental abilities of the family members. By arbitrarily assigning 30 units to adults and zero to a newborn, it is readily seen that the absence of a parent or the proliferation of close-together babies results in a lowered intellectual environment score. Zajonc points out that with the baby boom families nearly grown up, the family intellectual environment scores of young people who soon will be taking the SAT should rise—and so, he concludes, should the test scores.

Whether or not Zajonc is correct in his theory or his predictions, Tavris' concluding comment has a good deal of merit:

> Failure is an orphan, but success has a thousand parents. If SAT scores indeed increase by 1980, every jurisdiction will claim credit. City X will attribute the upswing to their open schools, and city Y will praise their unflinching attack on permissiveness. Educator A will pat himself on the back for his summer-school program, and educator B will pass the champagne to everyone involved in her "back-to-the-basics" approach (p. 74).

The most interesting point, of course, is that the data grinders will know that city X, city Y, educator A and educator B are each at least partly wrong in their claims. Conversely, each of these cities and educators will know in their more rational moments, even if test scores are rising, that the tests have not really measured the unique attributes and goals of their individual educational programs.

To summarize, the data clearly are not all in. The measurement and interpretation problems in standardized testing have not all been solved. Further, the data needs of program developers and users (including students) are not being fully met through achievement testing. Unfortunately, too much attention to falling standardized test scores may continue to distract us from other pressing educational issues.

Examining a Different Issue

In much of the current literature on declining test scores, one issue is frequently present, either implicitly or explicitly. It is the issue of "what should be done about school learning to insure higher scores on test taking?" In the present section, we would like to suggest that a significantly different issue should begin to command the time, energy and resources of educational leaders— the issue of "what should be done about school learning to insure more effective *in-life behaving*?" Two corollary problems involve (1) defining the kinds of school programs that relate directly to in-life usage, and (2) developing appropriate strategies for measuring the effects of such life-based programs. Before we move to a discussion of our new issue and its corollary problems, however, let us take one further look at some data—data that are different than that reviewed thus far.

The Relationship Between Academic Success and In-Life Success*

The data that are *not* available here are nearly as significant as those that are. We assume that some yet unknown threshold grasp of communicative and quantitative facts is essential to life success. Beyond that assumption, many researchers apparently have made the great leap of faith that school success is directly related to life success, so much so that comparatively little research effort has been turned toward investigating the nature and extent of this relationship. For example, our look at the literature revealed literally thousands of studies on "academic achievement," but only a handful of ERIC citations were found when "academic achievement" was paired with "professional recognition." No studies were found when the descriptors of "standardized tests" and "prognostic tests" each were paired with "professional recognition." Other pairings of similar descriptors also were used, all of which resulted in a relatively small number of applicable studies. A representative sample of these is reviewed below.

---

*We are using the phrase "in-life success" rather than "occupational success" in order to avoid excluding those life roles for which remuneration is not received but which, in the last analysis, may be fully as important to both men and women as is success on the job.

In discussing the role of the public schools in our society and the relationship of schools to the reinforcement of social class differences among people, Clasby (1976) cited the conclusions of McClelland (1974) as follows:

> Being a high school or college graduate gave one a credential that opened up. certain higher level jobs, but the poorer students in high school or college did as well in life as the top students.

Taylor (1971) reached a similar conclusion as a result of his research on creativity and other high level talents needed for adult life-effectiveness. He stated:

> For nearly two decades we have been searching for procedures to identify persons who will be effective during their professional careers, using a career criterion-oriented measurement approach. Early we discovered that grades, though expensively obtained through four college years, were of little value or even at times of no value whatsoever in spotting those who would be most successful as physicians, scientists, engineers, teachers, nurses and executives. It seems as if there are two different worlds, essentially lowly related or unrelated, namely the academic world and the professional career world (p. 7).

In March, 1974, the Research and Development Division of the American College Testing Program published its *ACT Research Report No. 62*. The authors, Munday and Davis (1974), reviewed and extended prior ACT research reports on the relationship between academic success and in-life success. In summarizing prior reports, they stated the following:

> Put simply, the research by Holland, Richards, Hoyt and their colleagues seems to demonstrate that success in school work is not related to success outside of school. Further it implies that academic talent may be only one kind of talent, and of limited consequence in the real world (p. 2).

Other researchers (Coppedge, 1969; Cox, 1971; Hoyt, 1966; Muchinsky and Hoyt, 1973; Pucel, 1972; and Thorndike, 1963) who investigated the relationship between selected measures of academic success and various scales of in-life success also found a general lack of relationship between the two.

If academic success is not related to life success, then to what is it related? Academic success is related to other forms of academic success. For example, according to Munday and Davis (1974), scores on achievement tests such as the SAT and the ACT "can be helpful in predicting college grades, but not college out-of-class accomplishments or probably not significant later-life accomplishments" (p. 12). (Other writers who also support this conclusion include Marland [1976] and Richards and Lutz [1967].) In fact, the predictive power of achievement tests in academic areas is basic to their use and validation.

In summary, test scores generally do not correlate with measures of in-life success. This is true for a number of reasons, the most prominent of which is that there are many other kinds of talent in addition to academic talent, and these other talents, either separately or in combination, appear to be the critical ones in determining life success.

The Goals and Content of
Life-Based Instructional Programs

Have the broad goals that should guide educational programs changed for the fourth quarter of the twentieth century? Probably not. Rather, has the complexity of everyday life increased to the extent that these goals must be approached *directly* and in selected non-traditional ways by schools? Probably yes. It is evident from the preceding research that a well-developed diversity of talent is required for in-life success today. It follows, therefore, that schools should offer broad programs that allow such diversity to blossom.

Stated in the most general terms, a long-standing goal of education has been, and is, *to assist people in becoming capable of effective and rewarding living.* Few would argue with the fact that this is a worthy goal of education, but somewhere along the line this goal is usually replaced with the goal of learning a specific body of information, coupled with the belief that mere possession of such information somehow later results in people leading effective and rewarding lives.

Life-based educational programs are an attempt to reinstate this goal of making people capable of effective and rewarding living, and to approach the goal directly rather than indirectly. A direct approach involves *practicing the varied behaviors that comprise the goal of effective living.* This places great importance on the learner's ability (1) *to establish personal goals for himself,* and (2) *to select and use means for reaching those goals.* Obviously, programs containing such humanistic breadth must include provisions for various aspects of the goals and behaviors of *each* student as well as the social relationships *among* students and other members of society.

Three Specific Life-Based Goals. Three specific educational goals that are operative at the classroom level of life-based schools are directly traceable to the broad goal of effective living outlined above. These three goals give direction (1) to the whole school enterprise, and (2) to the extremely important activity of evaluating the results of that school enterprise. In brief, the three more specific goals for students in life-based programs are as follows:

(1) to be able to make decisions regarding one's goals and actions so that these goals and actions lead to satisfying personal results, both now and later;

(2) to make these decisions in ways that are considerate of and helpful to other persons; and

(3) to be able to utilize the environment competently in carrying out both of the above actions.

Curricular Content for Life-Based Goals. If the three goals just listed are genuinely to provide direction for the curricular content of life-based schools, then the usual academic areas must give way to other ways of organizing content. Examples of other views of content are given below.

Content for Goal No. 1: Learning Processes. Learning processes in school must match what people do and how they learn throughout their lives. In our research, we have identified three learning processes—*issue resolving* (leading to the establishment of a goal), *product making* (leading to a desired object or event) and *open and focused inquiring* (leading to knowledge and competence). What these in-life processes are called in one program or another, however, is much less important than that they be operationalized for effective teaching, learning and evaluating.

Content for Goal No. 2: Attributes of the Learning Processes. At least three essential attributes may be identified within the learning processes of life-based programs. The first of these is a favorable self-concept that provides or develops student *confidence*. Some critical categories of behavioral evidence for this attribute include the following:

- the student initiates and executes the basic learning actions (learning processes);
- the student accepts and performs responsible roles; and
- the student expresses self-confidence and expectations of success.

A second attribute may be called *considerateness*, for which the following categories of evidence may be operationalized:

- the student refrains from disruptive behaviors;
- the student cooperates with others in the use of space and resources;
- the student treats others courteously; and
- the student respects the feelings and values of others.

And, finally, a third attribute of the learning processes engaged in by the student is that he or she exercises *rational commitment*. This attribute includes the following categories of evidence:

- the student chooses his or her own values and goals;
- the student makes choices rationally; and
- the student elects to conform to minimal rules of conduct, both in and out of school.

Obviously, one does not "teach" a favorable self-concept, considerateness or rational commitment. Rather, the life-based school creates conditions in which these attributes are rewarded and grow. Both the conditions and the individual student growth patterns are prime candidates for improved evaluation strategies.

Content for Goal No. 3: The Environment. Learning processes must be practiced continuously to develop competence in all areas of life or, to use another term, the environment. In our research, we have chosen to divide the environment on the basis of the natural laws that govern the manner in which things in the environment "behave" when behaved upon. Regardless of the details of such categories, all life-based programs are attempting to bring about learner-environment transactions designed to support "in-life competence" in addition to strictly "subject matter knowledge." We are using "knowledge" here to mean the mental images of environmental substances as well as the meanings and feelings that the student gives to those images. By "competence," we mean what the learner can do with those environmental substances for achieving his or her own goals. Finally, by "environmental substances," we mean oneself as well as all other persons, both natural and manmade physical things, all of the institutionalized artifacts of mankind's design (including language), and all of the things that are used for communicating, quantifying and bringing beauty into one's environment. This, in very broad brush strokes, is a potential organizational scheme for the subject matter content of the life-based curriculum. This content becomes real as students choose their goals with appropriate guidance from teachers and parents, and purposefully use learning processes in the achievement of their goals.

Strategies for Evaluating
Life-Based Programs

In this final section, we will examine briefly a basis for evaluating life-based educational programs. It will focus on a comprehensive concept of behavior.

A Definition of Behavior. If one is concerned primarily with problems of *measurement*, one may wish to establish a limited concept of behavior by ruling out of it any covert (i.e., unobservable by direct processes) or difficult to observe behavior.

It is possible, however, if one starts with a concern *directed first to educational goals of all dimensions*, to define behavior to include even those processes that are unobservable by direct means or difficult to observe. This increases the measurement problems, and also the instructional design problems, but it is worth the cost.

We recognize the rather formidable demands such a position poses. Nevertheless, in designing an evaluation plan for life-based programs, we assume that behavior consists of *any act* a person can perform on something in his environment for the purpose of exploring that environment or for using it in some way to reach some goal. Thus, behavior may be thought of as follows:

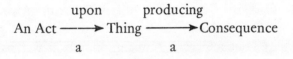

The "things" in our definition of behavior have already been expanded upon in generic form in a preceding section, titled "Goal No. 3: The Environment." Regarding the "acts" in our definition of behavior, we have identified four kinds that are involved in a life-based view of behavior, as follows:

Type I.   Non-verbal (hypothetical) mental processes that direct any observable actions in which a person might engage and that record the feedback from those overt actions.

Type II. Observable verbal expressions of Type I processes.

Type III. Observable but non-verbal manipulative kinds of actions that are expressions of Type I decisions.

Type IV. Sensate consuming acts (of particular concern in the fine arts), such as absorbing, identifying with, empathizing with and responding contemplatively to something.

Any complete behavior as defined above is an orchestration of these four types of responses or actions. All the ranges of scope that are essential to a full educational program are operative within these four types of responses, especially when their manifold interrelationships are kept in mind.

We regard this view of behavior to be a behaviorist position because the central notion of behaviorism is the analysis of behavior (or reduction of behavior) into three term contingencies (stimulus, response and consequences). This is a very sound and useful scheme. It does not *in itself* limit behavior to overt responses that can be observed and measured, nor does it limit learning processes to those of classical or operant conditioning.

Such limits are sometimes imposed by researchers, technologists and practitioners who find such delimitation appropriate to their tasks. However, life-based programs generally work with a broader definition of behavior. Such programs frequently attempt to deal with behavior in behavioristic terms where possible, although certainly departing from a strict behavioristic view when speaking of or attempting to validate hypothetical mental processes.

Working within the limits of sound research methodology, therefore, life-based program developers often ascribe to behavior some covert processes that are especially important to the more complex and creative range of human responses. All that is required is a little more ingenuity in dealing with the more difficult process of postulating those variables in the form of some useful construct, and in learning to assess the effects of those variables on overt and measurable responses. This is an old and profitable way of prenetrating nature.

Relationships Among Behavior, Practice and Evaluation. The principle that should guide the relationships among behavior, practice and evaluation in any teaching-learning model, including life-based programs, is that *people learn what they practice*. For this reason, it is our position that *evaluation* in life-based programs must be congruent with both the *behavior* that is desired and the *practice* of that behavior.

Thus, for example, if the behavior that we want the student to exhibit is issue resolving behavior, then we must engage the student in the *practice* of this very behavior. And our *measurement* of the student's issue resolving abilities must be accomplished by engaging him in issue resolving activities and then observing the processes he employs and the artifacts he produces while engaged in the activities. If, on the other hand, the behavior we are after is that of *verbalizing* about the processes of issue resolving, then this is what we must have the student practice and what we must have him do when measurement time comes. The two are distinctly different behaviors.

Summary

An understanding of the congruency among *behavior, practice* and *evaluation* is essential to the development of productive measures of achievement. To completely discard standardized tests will not solve our measurement problems. We simply will have lost a tool for measuring some kinds of behavior.

S.G. Sava (1975), I/D/E/A Executive Director, stated that our educational goals must "include not only the basic communication skills we need but also other things that enable human beings to get along in this world." He concluded, "I just can't believe that it's as simple as taking an exam" (p. 16). Valid and reliable measures of a much more complete range of human behavior are sorely needed so that carefully specified learning outcomes, including those that are measured by traditional tests, can be evaluated.

Increased awareness of and interest in the broad range of life-based learning outcomes may indeed result from the current testing controversy. If so, then students and all of society will be the obvious winners.

References

Clasby, M. Balancing the Social Cost/Benefit Scales of Testing. *Citizen Action in Education*, March 1976, *3*, 3-4.

Coppedge, F.L. Relation of Selected Variables from High School Records to Occupational and College Success. *The Journal of Educational Research*, October 1969, *63*, 71-73.

Cox, S.G. Do Educational Measures Predict Vocational Success? *Vocational Guidance Quarterly*, 1971, *19*, 271-273.

Green, R.L. Tips on Educational Testing: What Teachers and Parents Should Know. *Phi Delta Kappan*, 1975, *57*, 89-93.

Harnischfeger, A. and D.E. Wiley. *Achievement Test Score Decline: Do We Need to Worry?* St. Louis: CEMREL, Inc., 1975.

Harnischfeger, A. and D.E. Wiley. Achievement Test Scores Drop. So What? *Educational Researcher*, March 1976, *5*, 5-12.

Houts, P.L. Standardized Testing in America, II. *The National Elementary Principal*, July/August 1975, *54*, 2-3.

Hoyt, D.P. College Grades and Adult Accomplishment: A Review of Research. *Educational Record*, Winter 1966, *47*, 70-75.

I/D/E/A. *The Decline in Achievement*. Dayton: I/D/E/A, 1975.

Kohn, S.D. The Numbers Game: How the Testing Industry Operates. *The National Elementary Principal*, July/August 1975, *54*, 11-23.

Maehr, J. Schools Are Slipping. *Today's Education*, March/April 1976, *65*, 8.

Marland, S.P., Jr. Societal Issues: The Decline in National Test Scores. *ASCD News Exchange*, February 1976, *18*, 6-7.

McClelland, D.C. Testing for Competence Rather Than Intelligence. *The New Assault on Equality: I.Q. and Social Stratification*. A. Gartner, C. Greer and F. Riessman (Eds.) New York: Harper and Row, 1974, pp. 163-197, as quoted in Clasby, M. Balancing the Social Cost/Benefit Scales of Testing. *Citizen Action in Education*, March 1976, *3*, 3-4.

Muchinsky, P.M. and D.P. Hoyt. Academic Grades as a Predictor of Occupational Success Among Engineering Graduates. *Measurement and Evaluation in Guidance*, July 1973, *6*, 93-103.

Muller, S. American Education Standards Are Slipping. *Today's Education*, November/December 1975, *64*, 50-52.

Munday, L.A. and J.C. Davis. *ACT Research Report No. 62: Varieties of Accomplishment After College—Perspectives on the Meaning of Academic Talent*. Iowa City: The American College Testing Program, 1974.

NEA. Standardized Tests Must Go, Herndon Says. *NEA Reporter*, February 1976, *15*, 12.

NSTA. Conference on Standardized Testing. *NSTA News-Bulletin*, February 1976, 2.

Perrone, V. Alternatives to Standardized Testing. *The National Elementary Principal*. July/August 1975, *54*, 96-101.

Perrone, V. Better Ways Than Tests? *Citizen Action in Education*, March 1976, *3*, 7 and 12.

Pucel, D.J. *et al. The Ability of Standardized Test Instruments to Predict Training Success and Employment Success*. Minneapolis: Department of Trade and Industrial Education, University of Minnesota, 1972.

Rafferty, M. Teachers Blamed On Tests. *The Salt Lake Tribune*, February 1, 1976, p. 5.

Richards, J.M. and S.W. Lutz. *Predicting Student Accomplishment in College from the ACT Assessment*. Iowa City: The American College Testing Program, 1967.

Sava, S.G. Discussion. *The Decline in Achievement*. Dayton: I/D/E/A, 1975.

Stake, R.E. Societal Issues: The Decline in National Test Scores. *ASCD News Exchange*, February 1976, *18*, 6-7.

Tavris, C. After the Baby Boom . . . The End of the IQ Slump. *Psychology Today*, April 1976, *9*, 69-74.

Taylor, C.W. *Igniting Creative Potential*. Salt Lake City: Project Implode, 1971.

Thorndike, R.L. The Prediction of Vocational Success. *Vocational Guidance Quarterly*, 1963, *11*, 179-187.

Wilhelms, F.T. What About Basic Standards? *Today's Education*, November/December 1975, *64*, 46-48.

6.

Is a Lack of Instructional Validity Contributing to the Decline of Achievement Test Scores?

John F. Feldhusen, Kevin Hynes
and Carole A. Ames

Problem Statement

Academic achievement test scores are declining among American students at the junior and senior high school levels. Recently, several popular reports on the decline in achievement scores have appeared (Angoff, 1975; Babcock, 1974; Hechinger, 1974; Scully, 1975; Winkler, 1975). Because of the widespread concern about declining achievement scores, the College Entrance Examination Board and Educational Testing Service appointed an Advisory Panel to "assess the reasons for the dramatic drop in scores. . ." (Winkler, 1975, p. 10). Breland (1976) reviewed research on the SAT score decline for the Panel and asserted that factors specific to the tests themselves, such as scaling and test composition; factors influencing the examinee population, such as, race, sex and socioeconomic status; and factors associated with the schools, such as curricular changes, may all be contributing to the decline.

Harnischfeger and Wiley (1976) also reviewed research on the problem and concluded that the decline may be related to a number of factors, notably a decreased number of high school

John F. Feldhusen is Professor of Education and Psychology and Assistant Dean for Instructional Development, Purdue University, West Lafayette, Indiana. Kevin Hynes recently completed his doctorate in educational psychology at Purdue. Carole A. Ames is a graduate student in educational psychology at Purdue.

dropouts, increased absentee rates among students, decreased enrollments in academic courses, increased television viewing and changed family structures. They also suggested that the decline *cannot* be attributed to test artifacts, such as changes in test forms or norms.

Although there has been some discussion of test-specific problems that may be contributing to the decline, and assurance that these problems do not account for the decline in achievement, we believe that the tests cannot be exonerated quite so easily. A problem remains, inherent in standardized achievement tests; that problem concerns the validity of achievement tests for assessing the outcomes of instruction. Validation of standardized achievement tests typically focuses on content or curricular validity. However, content or curricular validity is not sufficient for assessing the validity of achievement tests, because this approach specifies the knowledge domain or the instructional objectives but fails to account for the realities of the instructional process.

A Proposal

Since traditional conceptions of validity are not sufficient for assessing the validity of achievement tests, we are proposing a new concept, *instructional validity*. A test is instructionally valid if (1) the knowledge or performance domain has been specified, and (2) it can be shown that well-conceived instruction has been provided for the attainment of each objective related to the knowledge or performance domain. The second condition implies two criteria: first, that instruction be of sufficient quality to assure an opportunity to learn; and, second, that it match the behavioral specifications of the objectives.

Content validity assures that the tested behaviors are a representative sample of a prespecified performance domain and that the performance domain has been defined adequately in terms of the desired outcomes (Davis, 1974). The concept of instructional validity subsumes the requirements of content validity but also requires that the student have an opportunity to learn the behavior that is being tested. For example, an essay test of a student's ability to synthesize ideas is of questionable instructional validity if the student has had no practice in organizing ideas or writing essays. A test has instructional validity when the learning objectives have been specified, when prior opportunities to learn those objectives have been provided to the student, and when the behavioral conditions of learning match the behavioral demands of the test items.

Opportunity to learn is a complex, multifaceted concept which, in the end, must be defined empirically. To say that a student has had an adequate opportunity to learn a set of behaviors may involve such activities as (1) exposing the student to essential information; (2) providing "quality" instruction as discussed by Bloom *et al.* (1971) within the context of "mastery learning" (e.g., sequence of presentation, presentation format, mode of instruction, etc.); (3) offering opportunities for appropriate practice of behaviors to be learned; and (4) providing corrective or reinforcing feedback. Other dimensions of opportunity to learn may imply a variety of methods for presenting the content, procedures to facilitate modeling of certain behaviors, and provisions for retention and transfer of learning. Whether or not a student has had an adequate opportunity to learn a behavior or skill is dependent upon the appropriateness of prior instruction.

In essence, an instructionally valid test is based upon specification of the skills to be measured within a performance domain and of the necessary instructional processes that produce learning. Instructional validity expands the concept of content validity by defining more precisely what constitutes a performance domain of behaviors that can be assessed. That is, for a behavior to belong to the performance domain, the student must have had an opportunity to learn that behavior. Thus, instructional validity is concerned with the instructional process and with determining the adequacy of the instructional procedures in relation to the assessed behaviors. A test is valid if the conditions of instruction were of sufficient *quality* and *matched* the performance specifications of the behavioral objectives.

Quality of Instruction

According to Carroll (1963) the quality of instruction is one of the principal factors affecting school learning. Although Carroll suggested that the quality of instruction depended upon the presentation, explanation, and sequencing of instruction, he provided very little guidance concerning ways to assess the quality of instruction.

The mastery learning model, developed by Bloom *et al.* (1971) and based on the Carroll model (1963), also emphasizes quality of instruction as it relates to the individual learner. Unfortunately, quality of instruction has been defined in a circular manner as follows: instructional quality is adequate if a student learns successfully from it. Furthermore, this definition applies only to the individual student and is not sufficient for group instruction.

Empirical procedures for evaluating instructional quality are now becoming available and are an outgrowth of the movement for educational product development (Baker and Schutz, 1971). These procedures provide evidence which indicates that evaluated material, methods and/or systems of instruction, will, if used according to specifications, produce learning. This evidence, then, provides guidance in a given testing situation. If the test is used following instruction with the evaluated materials, methods and/or system; if it can be shown that the performance domain had been adequately sampled; and if the instructional objectives match the behavioral demands of the test items, it might then be asserted that the achievement test had "instructional validity."

Matching Test Behaviors
with Instruction

The concept of a close match among the behavioral specifications of the objectives, test items and intervening instruction has been discussed by Mager (1973). Mager refers to the process as *Measuring Instructional Intent*, the title of his book. The common element among the behavioral objective, the instructional activity, and the test items is specifiable, observable behavior. Instruction must be focused on the behavior to be learned, and should include such activities as guidance, modeling, practice and corrective or reinforcing feedback.

Other Approaches to Validity

Criterion-referenced testing (CRT) was developed, in part, as an aid in constructing instructionally valid tests (Anderson *et al.*, 1975, p. 100). Sanders and Murray (1976) have also offered distinctions among criterion-referenced, norm-referenced, objectives-referenced, and domain-referenced tests. In a CRT approach, behavioral outcomes or abilities are specified, as well as acceptable levels of performance for mastery learning, and there is no normative differentiation among examinees. It is argued that in the norm-referenced approach to test development, the test is structured to assure that differential levels of performance are exhibited without consideration of what was or was not learned. Thus, factors that are not relevant to the instruction enter the assessment procedure and influence test results. In an instructionally valid test, however, items are coordinated with the behavioral objectives and the instructional procedures.

Shoemaker (1975) presented an approach to achievement testing which comes close to, and in several ways goes beyond, the concepts presented in this article. He stated his thesis as follows:

> The framework for achievement testing presented here necessitates a new philosophy towards the goals of an instructional program. At the core of this philosophy is the relationship between an item universe and an instructional program. Stated most succinctly, an instructional program and its associated item universe are isomorphic (p. 28).

Shoemaker goes on to assert that the ideal achievement test should be developed simultaneously with the instructional program(s) for which it is appropriate. The discussion which follows in his review focuses mostly on item universes and item domains. However, a major inference that can be made from the Shoemaker review is that a test is valid if it is specifically related to an instructional program which has in turn been developed to assure high or adequate quality of instruction for the universe of behavioral objectives associated with it.

Instructional Validity and the Decline
in Achievement Scores

Standardized achievement tests have content validity when their test behaviors sample a given performance domain; they have instructional validity when their performance domain is based on instruction that provided students an adequate opportunity to learn the performance to be tested. Historically, it has just been assumed that standardized achievement tests have instructional validity and that their performance domain reflected the instructional processes that occurred. We propose that instructional validity cannot be assumed but needs to be assessed; and that violation of the assumption of instructional validity may be contributing to the recently observed decline in achievement test scores.

Achievement test scores may have declined, *in part*, because the performance domains sampled by the tests do not accurately reflect the instructional processes that are occurring in schools. Changes in school curricula may be reflected chiefly in new instructional materials and methods which do not fit the preexisting objectives. The achievement test may possess validity in relation to the objectives but not in relation to the instructional procedures. Productive and worthwhile learning may be occurring, but the tests are declining in instructional validity and thus do not assess what is being learned.

Operationalizing Instructional Validity

One approach to assessing instructional validity is to adapt

Figure 1

Specifications for a Test on Classification of Isolating Mechanisms

Content Outline	Knowledge	Comprehension	Application	Analysis	Synthesis	Evaluation
I. Pre-Mating Mechanisms						
A. Seasonal and habitat isolation						
B. Ethological isolation						
C. Mechanical isolation						
II. Post-Mating Mechanisms						
A. Gametic mortality						
B. Zygotic mortality						
C. Hybrid inviability						
D. Hybrid sterility						

the standard test specification chart to include an assessment of instructional validity. Levels of objectives can be listed along the horizontal axis, and the performance domain can be outlined along the vertical axis. These two dimensions are sufficient for the assessment of content validity. In order to assess instructional validity, an additional dimension is needed. This can be provided by including a small box in the corner of each cell. This small box is used to record an assessment of the presence or absence of an instructional activity (1) which is of sufficient quality for students to achieve the specified outcome, and (2) which is appropriate for the behavioral demands of the test items. See Figure 1.

The evaluation of instructional validity may require a combination of judgments from curriculum coordinators, teachers, and/or principals. Ideally the evaluation will be based on an observation of the quality and behavioral appropriateness of the instruction which precedes the test, item by item. The classroom teacher should be able to contribute to this process by making judgments concerning the quality of instruction antecedent to each item and the behavioral match between test items and instructional activities. With help from a curriculum director and/or principal, teachers might be guided to examine the instructional activities offered in their classrooms in relation to the desired performance domain and types of instructional objectives. Such procedures should result in instructionally valid achievement testing.

Summary

We have argued that traditional concepts of test content validity are not adequate to assess the validity of an achievement test. A new concept, instructional validity, is needed. Instructional validity implies that a test is valid if it can be demonstrated that instruction of sufficient quality and behaviorally matched to the performance demands of the test items was offered. However, there is the problem that the concept of instructional validity may limit the assessment of validity to the level of the individual classroom, school or school system. We would argue, nevertheless, that far from being a problem, establishment of instructional validity at a local level would be highly desirable.

The current decline in academic achievement test scores may be due, in part, to the use of instructionally invalid tests. The concept of instructional validity, however, would be most difficult to apply in a national assessment. Perhaps the resolution will emerge from efforts at the state, regional and national levels of test development to ascertain generally the match of test items to the current realities of instruction. The effort might result in an imperfect assessment of instructional validity, but might be far better than our current tendency to ignore it.

References

Anderson, S.B., S. Ball, R.T. Murphy and Associates. *Encyclopedia of Educational Evaluation.* San Francisco: Jossey-Bass, 1975.

Angoff, W.H. Why the SAT Scores Are Going Down. *English Journal*, 1975, *65*, 10-11.

Babcock, B.B. Should We Really Wonder Why SAT Scores Are Going Down? *Independent School Bulletin*, 1974, *33*, 55-56.

Baker, R.L. and R.E. Schutz (Eds.) *Instructional Product Development.* New York: Van Nostrand-Reinhold, 1971.

Bloom, B.S., J.T. Hastings and G.F. Madaus. *Handbook of Formative and Summative Evaluation of Student Learning.* New York: McGraw-Hill, 1971.

Breland, H.M. The SAT Score Decline: A Summary of Related Research. A Report Prepared for the Advisory Panel on Score Decline. Princeton, New Jersey: Educational Testing Service, January 1976.

Carroll, J. A Model of School Learning. *Teachers College Record*, 1963, *64*, 723-733.

Davis, F.B. (Chair). *Standards for Educational and Psychological Tests.* Washington, D.C.: American Psychological Association, 1974.

Harnischfeger, A. and D.E. Wiley. Achievement Test Scores Drop. So What? *Educational Researcher*, 1976, 5, 5-12.

Hechinger, F.M. SAT Scores: What Happened to the Best and the Brightest? *Saturday Review World*, 1974, *1*, 65.

Mager, R.F. *Measuring Instructional Intent.* Belmont, California: Fearon, 1973.

Sanders J.R. and S.L. Murray. Alternatives for Achievement Testing. *Educational Technology,* 1976, *16*(3), 17-23.

Scully, M.G. Crackdown on Grade Inflation. *The Chronicle of Higher Education,* 1975, *11*(15), 1, 12.

Shoemaker, D.M. Toward a Framework of Achievement Testing. *Review of Educational Research,* 1975, *45,* 127-147.

Winkler, K.J. Panel to Probe Decline in College Board Scores. *The Chronicle of Higher Education,* 1975, *11*(8), 10.

7.

Minorities, Instructional Objectives and the SAT

Richard W. Burns

In light of the general decline in wide-range achievement and scholastic aptitude examination scores over the past few years in the United States, it is necessary to consider all causative possibilities or factors which contribute to score magnitude. Two factors, (1) who is taking the test, and (2) the relationship between test objectives and school objectives, are the subject of concern in this article.

El Paso Score Data

Using data from the El Paso Independent School District, there is evidence relating to population characteristics, which are often considered as factors influencing College Entrance Examination Board (CEEB) scores.* For the school years 1973-74 and 1974-75, data as revealed by the descriptive questionnaire completed by the testees show at least two changes which theoretically could be influencing the scores; namely, sex and ethnicity.

In the El Paso ISD the number and percent of graduates who took the Scholastic Aptitude Test (SAT) in the last two years were:

*All data in this article have been drawn from *Summary of Admission Testing Program of College Entrance Examination Board College Bound Seniors 1974-75*; a report of the El Paso Public Schools Department of Evaluation, Research and Planning; November, 1975.

Richard W. Burns is Professor of Education, University of Texas, El Paso.

Year	No. of All Graduates	Graduates Taking the SAT	
		No.	%
73-74	3761	1431	38
74-75	3976	1610	40

Of the above, the proportion of female testees increased the second year and, in fact, the number of females exceeded the males—which is in conformity with a national trend. Since traditionally males and females score differentially on the verbal and mathematics subtests, it follows that the SAT scores would change (perhaps decline) without there being a necessary decline in real quality of educational achievement. These facts are reflected in the numbers of students by sex taking the SAT in the El Paso ISD in the same two year period as:

Year	Number Taking SAT		Total
	Male	Female	
73-74	755	676	1431
74-75	800	810	1610

El Paso has an extremely high percent of minority students (many speaking English as a second language) as compared to the national and State of Texas average as reflected in Table 1. This minority composition is also reflected in economic factors. Although the average parental income between 1973-74 and 1974-75 rose approximately 11 percent locally, the percent of students expecting parental contributions to their education of less than $625 increased about 14 percent. Additionally, the average parental income of the El Paso sample remained substantially below that for the state and the nation; see Table 2.

The means of the Verbal and Mathematics scores on the SAT for local, state and national college bound seniors for the same two years is given in Table 3.

Table 1

*Percent of Minority Students
Taking Test*

Year	National	State	EPISD
73-74	14%	17%	42%
74-75	14%	18%	44%

The trend reflected in Table 3 is "down" for all three levels in the two year period, with a slightly larger percent change in the verbal as compared to the mathematics scores. Over a longer time span the decreases are even less, as reflected in Table 4.

In summary, the data tend to suggest that whereas the El Paso Independent School District SAT scores are below both state and national comparable scores, this can be accounted for by the large proportion of minority senior students taking the examination. According to the CEEB Guide, one should reasonably expect that students who speak English as a second language will have a handicap on the SAT in inverse proportion to their proficiency in English. Even though the number and percent of minority students taking the test has recently increased, the decline in the last four years is no more than might be expected by chance alone. Also, the changing composition of the test group relative to male-female proportions seems to have had little if any effect on the test scores. Theoretically, if a larger proportion of women are taking the test, one would expect a larger decline in mathematics as compared to the verbal scores; but, just the reverse has been true.

The Instructional Factor

From examining the local data, which show that the El Paso ISD seniors achieve scores which have in the past and which

Table 2

Financial Data
for Students Taking Test

Data	Year	National	State	EPISD
Average Parental Income	73-74	$17,563	$18,233	$13,855
	74-75	18,952	19,658	15,402
Expected Parental Contribution to Education Less than $625	73-74	26%	24%	38%
	74-75	38.5%	35.9%	54.4%

continue to compare favorably with scores of comparable groups, and that for all practical purposes there has been no major decline in the last four years, even with sex and minority changes in the population composition, one is inclined to have to turn to *other* reasons to account for the over-all decline in scores. This observation has led me to hypothesize that there is an *instructional factor* operating.

Without trying to detail all the reasons why—and they are numerous—I would like to suggest that the CEEB testing program, based on some unknown specific objectives, has not kept pace with the post World War II changes in the unknown specific objectives of the various educational systems. It is obvious to even the most casual observer that cultural mores and values have been undergoing tremendous reforms (shifts) in the United States. One only need to mention marriage-divorce, energy-transportation, youth-drug, economy-inflation, labor-unemployment, food-food fads, Vietnam War-activists, politics-Watergate, corporations-pay-offs (bribes), moral values-crime to get a notion of the upheavels and unrest, *with the concomitant changes in the expectations of youth from "schooling,"* to realize that students' objectives for

Table 3

Scholastic Aptitude Test
Comparison of Mean Scores for 1973-74, 74-75

Test	National		State		EPISD		EPISD % Change
	73-74	74-75	73-74	74-75	73-74	74-75	
Verbal	444	434	439	431	416	403	-3%
Mathematics	480	472	475	467	446	437	-2%
Number Taking Test	824,601	996,409	43,698	48,790	1,431	1,610	------------

learning may differ from the objectives on which the tests are based. Earlier I referred to the "unknown specific objectives" of both the tests and our local school systems. This is so because in neither case are the specific objectives specified in written form.* The lack of written objectives does not imply that either the test or school programs are objectiveless, because in either case there are implied objectives or indirect objectives specified by topics or curricular content.

Returning to the El Paso ISD as an example, there have been hundreds of curricular changes, some of major proportions over even the past 10 years. These changes have been brought about by public pressure, student activism, government projects, a changing social climate and a different economic environment, to mention a few of the major causes. The result has been a greater emphasis on drug education, family living, career education, bilingual educa-

*The El Paso ISD does have performance objectives in some subject areas and this facet of education is being increasingly implemented.

Table 4

Four-Year Summary of
Scholastic Aptitude Test Scores
for El Paso Independent School District

Subject Field	71-72	72-73	73-74	74-75	4 year % change
Verbal	415	413	416	403	-2.9
Mathematics	441	433	446	437	-0.9

tion, multi-cultural education, practical mathematics, contemporary novels, science fiction, newspapers (current events and problems), personal health problems and sex education, to enumerate a few topics from the content viewpoint. At the same time there has been a decided shift away from rote memory and textual learning to a greater emphasis on audio-visual instructional techniques; science taught as a process area; the use of newspapers as the source material for economics and other subject matter; instruction in both English and Spanish; the inclusion of source materials from many cultures; and a less formal atmosphere (civil rights, students rights, dress codes, etc.), all of which have affected the totality of instruction. It is not difficult to see how the test objectives could well have become more divergent as a list when compared to school instructional objectives. I say more divergent because there never was a one-to-one relationship.

This hypothesis of a discrepancy in specific objectives—that is, the SAT in fact has recently been measuring less well *what has been taught*—is impossible to substantiate because of the *lack of written performance standards*. The CEEB program should be based on specific objectives, made public; and school districts should make public the objectives of instruction at all levels in all areas. The one-to-one relationship (overlap) of the CEEB tests'

objectives and the local educational objectives will be the degree
to which the tests, such as the SAT, are valid measures of local
educational achievement. When such lists are available, then and
only then, will it be possible to interpret gains or declines in test
scores in some sensible manner.

I personally believe the long range decline in SAT scores has
been as much a reflection of increased divergence between what
has been measured and what has been learned as any other factor;
although other factors may *also* be operating. This implies neither
a criticism of the tests per se nor the local school district
educational efforts. It merely says: "they (the tests and the
educational effort) have most likely been increasingly different for
some rather long but unknown period of time."

8.

Has the Key to the Mystery of Drops in Standardized Test Scores Been Discovered?

John M. Throne

Recent declines in scores on tests of achievement per se, and on tests functionally if not conceptually indistinguishable from them, such as aptitude, intelligence, etc., "have spurred considerable public discussion and debate" (Harnischfeger and Wiley, 1976). Evidently it surprises no one that all these tests are correlated in their decline; each measures performances related to the same, single criterion: scholastic success. What puzzles some is the decline itself. The possible key to the mystery seems to have been overlooked. It is that the tests at issue, without exception, are *standardized*.

What is a standardized test? It is a measure of performance under standardized conditions. "Standardization implies *uniformity of procedure* in administering and scoring the test" (Anastasi, 1976, p. 25). "Another important step in the standardization of a test is the establishment of *norms*. . . tests have no predetermined standards of passing or failing; an individual's score is evaluated by comparing it with the scores obtained by others" (Anastasi, 1976, p. 26). "In the process of standardizing a test, it is administered to a large, representative sample of the type of subjects for whom it is designed. This group, known as the standardization sample, serves to establish the norms" (Anastasi, 1976, p. 26). "Any

John M. Throne is with the Bureau of Child Research at the University of Kansas, Lawrence.

norm . . . is restricted to the particular normative population from which it was derived . . . norms are in no sense absolute, universal or permanent . . . they . . . represent the test performance of the subjects constituting the standardization sample . . . in choosing such a sample, an effort is usually made to obtain a representative cross section of the population for which the test is designed (Anastasi, 1976, p. 89).

These remarks by Anne Anastasi provide the clue to why standardized scores on achievement and other tests have been declining in recent years. *The standardization samples on the basis of whose performances the test norms were established no longer represent the testees to whom the tests are applied.* The same point may be made the other way around. *The testees to whom the tests are applied are no longer represented by the standardization samples on the basis of whose performances the test norms were established.*

In other words, norms on standardized tests have been derived from performances of subject *samples* drawn from subject *populations* not now in existence. Therefore, what the recent decline in scores on standardized tests means is that, to the disadvantage of testees on those tests in the present, any basis for comparing their performances with the performances of the standardization samples and the populations they represented in the past has ceased to obtain; nor is it likely to obtain in the future. The basis for that comparison is simply a similar (though not necessarily an identical) set of testing circumstances: those identified by Anastasi in the aforementioned quotations defining standardized testing.

Implicit in Anastasi's definition are two assumptions that need to be made explicit. Because they are not explicit may be why the key to the mystery of declining standardized test scores may have been missed. In order for standardized tests to be said *with psychometric or educometric exactitude* to have been administered to testees, and scored, under similar circumstances (in the present), the testees (1) must have had experiences (in the past) and (2) must have experiences (in the future) similar to those of the tests' samples and their populations. Otherwise, to speak of *standardized* test administration is to be misleading.

It is true, as Anastasi makes clear, that "uniformity of procedure in administering and scoring" must prevail for testing to be standardized. It is also true, however, that if the previous history of the testees is different from instead of similar to a test's sample and population, it will be meaningless to administer that test to and score those testees through "uniform procedures." A testee tutored on the test items to perform as well as another testee not so tutored is an obvious case in point. To administer the test to and score the first testee using "uniform procedures" would be an example not of standardized but "pseudo-standardized" testing (or worse). By the same token, since the purpose of standardized testing is to predict, or at least project, how the testees will do outside of or after testing, it is also meaningless to test them with the "uniform procedures" called for by standardized testing unless it is known (or at least expected) that their subsequent history is to be more similar to than different from the samples' and populations' of the tests employed. For it is only if this is so that there will be any basis for such a prediction or projection. An apt illustration here is if the testees are fated to experience situations functioning to suppress their best performances, such as deprived educational environments, in contrast to samples and populations whose educational environments, stimulating or enriched, operate to express them.

But environments that are deprived, on the one hand, or stimulating or enriched, on the other, have relative, not absolute, effects. That is, what may work *to express*, for one subject under one set of conditions, may act *to suppress*, for another subject under other conditions. This might explain what mere differences as opposed to similarities of circumstances before and after (even if not during) testing do not: the *drop* in standardized test scores universally recorded lately, aside from their mere *change* (up as well as down). What presumptively should have resulted in an improved psycho-educational milieu in the last five to ten years because of quantum jumps in financial resources poured into school construction and programs, teachers' salaries, etc., may have had precisely the opposite result.

In any event, if educational effectiveness is to be judged by standardized test scores when these reflect unfavorably, too, not just favorably, upon the educational milieu, it must be conceded that the effectiveness of educational efforts has begun to evidence a downward trend. The reason may be that those presumptive psycho-educational improvements are an illusion; that *more* (money, teachers, etc.) has not proved to be *better*. Changed psycho-educational circumstances from those prevailing for standardization samples and their populations prior and subsequent to "uniform procedures of administration and scoring of tests," i.e., standardized testing narrowly defined, may account for changes in scores registered of late by testees on those tests. But the drops in the form of which those test score changes have occurred may have stemmed from the fact that those psycho-educational circumstances before and after standardized test administration and scoring have changed for the worse.

Thus the key to the mystery of (a) changed and (b) lowered standardized test scores may have been found.

References

Anastasi, A. *Psychological Testing*. New York: Macmillan, 1976.
Harnischfeger, A. and D.E. Wiley. Achievement Test Scores Drop. So What? *Educational Researcher*, 1976, 5, 5-12.

9.

Changing IQ and Family Context

Herbert J. Walberg

From large scale testing of draftees, it may be estimated that the average IQ score of the young adult male population rose about 20 points from World War I to 1960. The rise is probably attributable to improvements in nutrition, child rearing and education; declining numbers of children per family; population movement from rural to urban areas; and immigrants' mastery of the language on the tests (Walberg, 1974).

Analyses of scores in Minnesota, Michigan and Scotland from the same period show that the variation in IQ was increasing. Increasing heterogeneity of IQ is apparently attributable to increased assortative mating (the bright marrying bright and the dull marrying dull) and the IQ-stimulation which bright parents can more easily confer; propensities of adults in the upper and lower overlapping thirds of the IQ, income and education ranges to have more children than those in the middle thirds; concentration of the poor in urban areas of high crime; poor schools and broken families; and the mutual intensification of these factors (Walberg, 1974).

Since about 1960, as authors of other papers in this book show, the average ability and achievement of college applicants have been declining. Naturally parents, educators and others would like to know the reasons for the rise and fall.

Herbert J. Walberg is Professor of Human Development, University of Illinois at Chicago Circle, Chicago.

The data are spotty; and our understanding of the social, psychological and educational forces bearing on national IQ changes over extended periods is unclear. Nevertheless, evidence from different countries and going back to the 1920s shows that the quality of intellectual stimulation by the *family* accounts for a great deal of the variation in student abilities and achievements measured on standardized mental tests. Investigators have repeatedly shown that such indicators of family environment as the number of children in the home and the socioeconomic level of the parents weigh more heavily than variations in schooling, such as expenditures, class size and teacher characteristics in the determination of test scores (Walberg, 1974; Walberg and Marjoribanks, 1976). (Such evidence, by the way, should not be taken as an inegalitarian indictment of the schools; on the contrary, it indicates much greater equality of school opportunity than equality of family opportunity.)

The work of Zajonc and Markus, that won the American Association for the Advancement of Science Socio-Psychological Prize for 1975, shows that earlier increases in family size systematically account for much of the recent decline of the test scores among college applicants beginning about 1960. Zajonc (1976) also shows that decreases in family size since 1963 account for the rising scores of elementary school children since about 1970. It is very likely that by 1982 college applicant scores will be rising sharply because of the earlier large reductions in family size.

Family size and social class are, of course, crude indications of the IQ-stimulating qualities of the home. They account for about a quarter of the variance in student test performance. There are many exceptions, and bright children may be found in poor families and in large families. Fewer may be found in poor, large families, although there are exceptions even in these cases.

For a more precise estimate of the stimulating qualities of the home, structured interviews with parents have been developed (see Walberg, 1974, and Walberg and Marjoribanks, 1976, for a review of these techniques). Such interviews index the complexity of the parents' language, the amount of time spent interacting with a child, the quality of reinforcement of learning and related factors; over-all ratings of the family environment account for a half to three quarters of the variation on mental test scores. Ratings of these qualities account for more of the exceptional cases, parents of lower socioeconomic status or of large families who can afford or who take the time to enrich their children's intellectual development.

The family remains the crucible of intellectual development, and its qualities are the main determinants of intellectual, physical and emotional growth. None of this is to say that the schools cannot be improved nor that technology, medicine, welfare and other agencies of our culture have no role to play in enhancing the growth of IQ and other traits. To be sure they have.

References

Walberg, H.J. Optimization Reconsidered. In J. Walberg (Ed.) *Evaluating Educational Performance: A Sourcebook of Methods, Instruments and Examples.* Berkeley, California: McCutchan, 1974.

Walberg, H.J. and K. Marjoribanks. Family Environment and Intellectual Development. *Review of Educational Research*, 1976.

Zajonc, R.B. Family Configuration and Intelligence. *Science*, April 1976, *191*(16), 227-236.

10.

The Test Score Decline:
If You Don't Know Where You're Going,
How Do You Expect to Get There?

Robert M. Rippey

The various authors in this series of articles each have their own dominant theory explaining the decline in SAT and other test scores. I am sympathetic with many of the other explanations offered and I am certain that the explanation of the decline of scores is sufficiently complex to require a number of contending hypotheses. My own position is that schooling currently suffers from a confusion of aims.

I intend first to establish the existence of the confusion, secondly to suggest why the confusion might adversely affect test scores and finally to suggest what might be done to improve the prognosis.

Some Knew Where
They Were Going

The aims of schooling have not always been in doubt. Plato, in designing a curriculum for the leaders of his ideal state, says to Glaucon:

> ...I bethink myself that we certainly said, did we not, that our
> pupils must be trained in their youth to war? Yes, we did say so.
> Then the science which we are in quest ... can be turned to use
> by warlike men.

Robert M. Rippey is with the Department of Research in Health Education, University of Connecticut Health Center, Farmington, Connecticut.

The New England Primer left no doubts in the mind of the child about what he was supposed to achieve:

> In Adam's fall, we sinned all.
> Thy life to mend, this book attend.

The Great Depression inspired an aim of employability. The World War II schools promoted patriotism and service to country. And the age of Rickover urged each student to do his bit to outstrip the Russians in space technology. You would be correct in claiming that at least some of these aims of schooling were perhaps misguided and not done too well.

The Athenians lost in Sicily; not a few New Englanders went to Hell; not all of the class of '38 were employed; not all of the class of '44 stayed out of the black market; and not all of the class of '55 have been to the moon and back. For all that, their test scores (including SATs in our generation) weren't bad. At least so say the participants in the current fracas.

Perhaps the initial bit of evidence supporting my hypothesis that a confusion of aims about education is responsible for declining performance is the fact that we bring up the question of declining SAT scores at all. If, as Marland (1975) has said, the role of the SAT is to predict academic performance of students in colleges and universities and "...it still does well what it was originally intended to do," then why should we care if the scores go down as long as they (the scores) assure the sons of the brave their rightful place at fair Harvard? The fact that you, the reader, have pursued this series of articles to this point suggests that you may be suffering from a similar confusion of aims.

As a second demonstration of the current state of confusion, let me ask you to put this article down for a minute (don't forget to pick it back up, though) and write what you believe to be the aims of schooling through high school. Think about a specific child. Think about the future of that child and what he or she might become.

Did you write a rather long list? Ask several other friends to do the same task. Did your list agree with theirs? How much agreement did you find? When you get an opportunity, ask some persons you don't know so well to make out such a list also. Try to select someone different from yourself—a different sex, a different socioeconomic status or from a different part of the country. How is your agreement?

Now take your list and select the single objective you would retain if you had to give up all the others.

Was that a difficult task? Did it take you a while to decide? What did your friends do this time? Still not convinced? I have some data.

About three years ago I asked more than 100 children in a public elementary school a very simple question: What do you need to do to get a good grade in school? Not one of the students answered with anything related to learning. Their responses all dealt with being good, minding the teacher and keeping in one's seat. All admirable goals, but I don't think those aims appeared on either your list or mine.

In asking you to make out your list, I neglected something: the client. The student is often left out of planning. Goals are seldom shared with him. When goals are shared, they may not be in a form which he understands. If he does understand, his experiences with learning and with testing may convince him that the goals he was told about are not the true ones. In fact, the student is correct. There are at least two curricula in most schools: the one we talk about and the one which you have to figure out for yourself. This also has been documented eloquently by Mary Alice White (1967) in a study of over 1000 children in the New York City schools. Her conclusion was:

> The pupil has not a cognitive map of content to guide him through the labyrinth of knowledge he is asked to master . . . the map he does use . . . is the map of his school experience. His experiences in school are the organizers of his knowledge. That scheme is organized by the way in which the school life is organized, that is, by grade level, by subject, by teachers and by the daily schedule. Categories are built upon their location in school life. "We studied that in third grade, Miss X taught us that,

etc." The analogy that might make the pupil's view more comprehensible to adults is to imagine oneself on a ship, sailing across an unknown sea to an unknown destination. An adult would be desperate to know where he is going. But a child only knows that he is going to school, that he has absolutely no choice in the matter and that all the adults in his life have decided he is to make this voyage along with the other children he knows. The chart is neither available nor understandable to him. He does not even know how long the voyage will take. Very quickly, the life on board ship becomes all important. If it is highly organized, as school life is, this structure serves as a series of cubby holes into which he tucks those pieces of information he retains. The daily chores, the demands, the inspections become the reality, not the voyage, not the destination.

Two Curricula

Dreeben (1968) in his book *On What Is Learned in School*, provides additional insight from the sociological point of view into the source and function of the curriculum of the person and the curriculum of the institution. Dreeben concluded that schooling is designed to develop four basic attitudes; independence, achievement, universality and specificity. This means that students are to learn to (Dreeben, 1968, pp. 63):

(1) act by themselves . . ., (2) perform tasks actively and master the environment according to certain standards of excellence, (3) acknowledge the rights of others to treat them as members of categories, (4) on the basis of a few discrete characteristics rather than the full constellation . . . that represents the whole person.

Dreeben points out that the accomplishment of these objectives is an essential part of the transition between family life as a child and occupational life as an adult. If the child is to assume a productive role in modern industrial society, he is taught that he must be able to fit the mold. He must be able to abandon his quest for a personal identity and become an effective cog in the machinery of modern life. Yet, the aims of independence and achievement are somewhat at odds with the aims of universalism and specificity. He goes on to point out that universality and specificity are seldom regarded as good.

> Parents and teachers admonish children to do their own work
> well; few of them support the idea that people should acknowl-
> edge their similarity to one another in specifically categorical
> terms while ignoring their obvious differences.

In addition to the contrasting values placed on the first two
norms when compared with the last two, the logic of the two pairs
of norms is also in conflict. How does a young person cope with
the problem of being an achievement-oriented individual, yet
remain a member of a category ignoring individual differences?
Furthermore, Dreeben (p. 84) points out that each of the four
generally established aims of schooling contains an inherent
polarity.

> Potentialities for success and failure are inherent in tasks
> performed according to achievement criteria. Independence mani-
> fests itself as competence and autonomy in some, but as heavy
> burden of responsibility and inadequacy in others. Universalistic
> treatment represents fairness to some, cold impersonality to
> others. Specificity may be seen as situational relevance or
> personal neglect.

The last two goals, universality and specificity, in addition to
being less than well liked, are also never stated. They form part of
the latent curriculum of the school. Dreeben provides quite
convincing evidence that they nevertheless lurk. Their obscurity is
a defense. Yet, if one of the unstated aims of schooling is
mediocrity (universalism) under the guise of either democracy or
occupational adaptability, is it any wonder that children, who
have a real need for feelings of competence and acceptance, are
confused by the two conflicting curricula?

A Final Blow to Clear Aims

On top of the sometimes conflicting personal and institutional aims of school, a third conflicting source must be
added—the unresolved anxieties of parents. Perhaps the most
aleatory and damaging source of aims for schooling comes from
these unfulfilled expectations. This perversion of the aims of
schooling was eloquently described almost 20 years ago by

Erikson (1959). He was concerned with the need of the child to develop good feelings about himself by developing a sense of industry.

> Good teachers, healthy teachers, relaxed teachers, teachers who feel trusted and respected by the community understand . . . how to alternate play and work, games and study . . . Good parents, healthy parents, relaxed parents feel a need to make their children trust their teachers and therefore to have teachers who can be trusted.

The good teacher, to Erikson, helps the child to avoid three dangers.

> There is, first, the above mentioned sense of inferiority, the feeling that one will never be any good—a problem which calls for the type of teacher who knows how to emphasize what a child *can* do. Second, there is the danger of the child's identifying too strenuously with a too virtuous teacher or becoming a teacher's pet . . ., being nothing but a good little worker or a good little helper which may not be all he *could* be. Third, there is the danger that throughout the long years of school, he will never acquire the enjoyment of work and the pride of doing at least one kind of thing well . . . this is a socially decisive stage; since industry involves doing things beside and with others, a first sense of division of labor and equality of opportunity develops . . . When a child begins to feel that it is the color of his skin, the background of his parents, or the cost of his clothes rather than his wish and his will to learn which will decide his social worth, lasting harm may ensue for the sense of identity.

In opposition to the possible constructive aspects of schooling, Erikson also points toward the possibility of exploitation residing in the school situation. The length of childhood and the length of the schooling which goes with that long childhood contain both a promise and a threat:

> Human childhood is long so that parents and schools may have time to accept the child's personality in trust and to help it to be disciplined and human in the best sense known to us. This long childhood exposes the child to grave anxieties and a lasting sense of insecurity which, if unduly and senselessly intensified, persists in the adult in the form of vague anxiety . . . This long childhood exposes adults to the temptation of thoughtlessly and often cruelly exploiting the child's dependence by making him the

victim of tensions which we will not or dare not correct in ourselves or in our surroundings. We have learned not to stunt the child's growing body with child labor; we must now learn not to break his growing spirit by making him the victim of our anxieties.

And is not one of the greatest of the anxieties the one about school, and does not our anxiety over SAT scores point to the centrality of this anxiety? The current picture of anxious children of anxious parents, anxiously taught in anxious schools by anxious teachers does not portend growth.

The question may arise that since the authors quoted heretofore have mentioned the problem of confusion of aims as far back as 1959, why has the decline become more pronounced recently? My answer is that although Erikson was concerned about the problem early on, it became more pronounced, and more was written about the problem in the late 60s (Dreeben, 1968; Ehrlich, 1969; Jackson, 1968; White, 1968). Their observations were made primarily in conventional schools. Add to this the development of some programs of open schooling which did not fully understand the original British concept, and which relied primarily on chaos and disorder as a source of whatever objectives were discernible, and one sees a full fruition of aimlessness at about 1968. Some members of the class of '76 may be the first graduating class to have the benefits of 12 full years of aimless education.

Why Unclear Aims Debilitate

The reasons are clear. Energies are dispersed. Satisfaction in accomplishment is difficult when accomplishment is ill-defined. A source for motivation is lacking when there is no criterion for success. Reason for commitment is lacking when there is nothing to be committed *to*. Reciprocity cannot exist when there is nothing to which to reciprocate. And, finally, accountability for results becomes impossible: students can rightfully say that they didn't know what was expected of them, or whether in fact anything was expected of them. At this point, teachers can relax into the vagaries of artistry. However, the lack of clarity of aims of schooling is not totally disfunctional. In a pluralistic society, where many goals compete for the attention and resources of the school, the formulation of ill-defined goals which each person may read in his or her own way approaches an art form. Taking a cue from political speech writers and tobacco account ad men, some educators have learned to polish an obfuscation. Others assign curriculum committees the task of coming up with a list of objectives on which "everyone can agree." Without clearer guidance this can result in its own kind of vague doggerel. The benefits of such plastic prose are many: faculty can relax in the teachers' lounge, spending endless hours debating the meaning of these vacuities; administrators can claim successes without the slightest fear of being contradicted and children can get off the hook easily by telling their parents "I don't know what it means either—ask my teacher."

What Can Be Done?

You may counter with a statement "the 70s have been the age of objectives. After all, I've read Mager and so have you. I have spent many hours listing objectives for every one of my courses."

I'm sure you have. Unfortunately, that is not what I am concerned with. One can have a thousand and one specific behavioral objectives and still find that 1001 objectives are diffuse, confused or both. Each may be out of joint with the other. What I am talking about is not a plethora of things to do or to be able to do, but a dominant purpose or reason for devoting 12 or more years of one's life to otherwise non-productive activity.

Furthermore, no matter how many aims are in the syllabus, this has no effect if the aims are not shared with students. As an example, I recall helping to develop a program about six years ago for 12 young men who were in trouble with everyone. They classified themselves into two antagonistic groups, each group referring to the other group pejoratively as "greasers" or "hippies" although they never were quite able to distinguish what made the difference. Generally speaking, the hippies were perceived as having long hair, and a taste for Cat Stevens and dope. The greasers wore leather jackets, drank a lot and liked to fight. Their criminal activity was varied and imaginative, one member of the class getting arrested for the unusual offense of being an accessory to indecent exposure.

Now, in trying to arrive at a curriculum for them and with them, conflicts developed. Our objectives included graduating, staying out of jail, developing some job skills and learning how to get along with difficult people (such as mothers, fathers, brothers, sisters, teachers, other students, village officials and occasional innocent by-standers). Their objectives were explicit and universal. They wanted more information about booze, dope, women and money—and only the order varied. The information desired focused primarily on "where and how to get it." You can see the difficulty of reciprocity, yet reciprocity was not impossible. We tried, and our efforts were not futile. These 12 students, who had been predicted not to finish their first year, all graduated from high school, some served in the Army following graduation, some were employed and several are now in college. Unfortunately, two have died—one of an overdose and one in an auto accident. Many of these students who were expected to drop out come back after graduation to show off wives, babies, pets and cars to the students now enrolled. And, in 1976, most are much further along than anyone expected back in 1970; I imagine their SAT scores would be higher than anyone would have predicted.

One characteristic which distinguished this program was the clarity of its goals. They were written, articulate and meaningful. Although initially written for adults, the students understood the student version well. They could explain many of the goals in their own terms to anyone who asked.

An example of one of the program goals is: Given a difficult conflict situation in the classroom, the student will demonstrate an increased understanding of the behavior of others by: (1) being able to describe how the other person behaved, (2) being able to state why the other person behaved as he did and (3) explaining what message the behavior was trying to tell.

The students knew that this meant "If someone is angry at me, I ought to be able to figure out why." They also knew the meaning of this objective in terms of the behavior of the adults in the program who would try to explain their own feelings if they became angry. The goal was not the unrealistic one of not being angry, but only of understanding anger better.

Although I have illustrated one of the affective aims of the program, there were many cognitive aims as well. Some of the students did not wish to meet all of the aims of the program, and many were not of their own choosing. On the other hand, the program was pleasant, and a sufficient number of aims were acceptable enough that they persisted.

The difference between the external aims of the school and the internal aims of the student is not necessarily a bad thing; but such differences make reciprocity imperative. It is not necessary for the school and the child to be in perfect agreement about aims. They seldom are. If they were, school would probably be unnecessary. What is necessary is that the school and the teacher must have a clear idea of both general and specific institutional aims which can be conveyed to the child. Furthermore, to achieve the necessary reciprocity, the teacher must have a commitment to both understand and help clarify the personal aims of the child.

Why is reciprocity so important? First, because a school without reciprocity deprives the child of a basic experience in human relations. Adequate moral development cannot occur in the absence of experiences with reciprocity. Second, reciprocity is an important element of making school likeable. Why should school be likeable? Some research suggests that teaching according to student teaching style preference has little effect on achievement. You may point out a slight negative correlation between liking instruction and short term achievement. However, Ehrlich (1969) demonstrated that some poor achievers have an unrealistic and euphoric picture of school which is quite different from the realistic liking of the high achiever. Thus, the traditional low or negative correlation between liking and learning is a result of the confusion of authentic liking with "school euphoria."

The secret to long term learning is involvement and commitment, and that commitment is encouraged by liking. The cognitive psychologist, John Cotten (1973), puts it this way: "The rewards of participation in school (not just excelling, but day to day participation) must exceed the rewards of loafing and daydreaming." So we MUST make school a pleasant place to live (Montessori called schools "houses for children"), not because we are big, loveable humanists, but because that is a key way we can get people to learn. This means that we must make school rewarding not only to the stars of the show, but also to the ordinary plodders and good citizens, and even the bad guys.

The Moral Dimension of Curriculum Decison-Making

In deciding on the institutional aims of schooling, it is possible to take a number of positions which seem to fit rather nicely into Lawrence Kohlberg's levels of moral reasoning. Kohlberg has classified moral reasoning into six levels which he describes as shown in the first column of Table 1 (Turiel, 1973).

In reviewing the aims of schooling, it might be useful to classify the various suggested aims according to the level of moral reasoning they represent before taking a final vote. There is perhaps one other position which doesn't fall into the six categories because it is beyond the pale of morality, and that position says "Whatever it is, if it costs less, it is better." I would not mention the position if it were not so prevalent at the moment.

With the many possible positions regarding the aims of education, no wonder school programs seem aimless and no wonder children become confused and misdirect their energies.

Developing consensus on an appropriate set of aims may seem difficult, but it is indispensable. As a former colleague of

Table 1

Description of Level of Moral Reasoning	Example of This Stage of Reasoning in Curriculum Decision-Making
STAGE 1: The Punishment and Obedience Orientation. The physical consequences of action determine its goodness or badness regardless of the human meaning or value of these consequences. Avoidance of punishment and unquestioning deference to power are valued in their own right, not in terms of respect for an underlying model order supported by punishment and authority (the latter being Stage 4).	EXAMPLE 1: We must educate children or they will be animals and turn against us.
STAGE 2: The Instrumental-Relativist Orientation. Right action consists of that which instrumentally satisfies one's own needs and occasionally the needs of others. Human relations are viewed in terms like those of the market place. Elements of fairness, of reciprocity and of equal sharing are present, but they are always interpreted in a physical, pragmatic way. Reciprocity is a matter of "you scratch my back and I'll scratch yours," not of loyalty, gratitude or justice.	EXAMPLE 2: If I train my kids to be good and make a living, they will take care of me when I get old.
STAGE 3: The Interpersonal Concordance or "Good Boy-Nice Girl Orientation." Good behavior is that which pleases or helps others and is approved by them. There is much conformity to stereotypical images of what is majority or "natural" behavior. Behavior is frequently	EXAMPLE 3: If I work for the schools it will look good. My mother would like it.

judged by intention—"he means well" becomes important for the first time. One earns approval by being "nice."

STAGE 4: The Law and Order Orientation. There is orientation toward authority, fixed rules and the maintenance of the social order. Right behavior consists of doing one's duty, showing respect for authority and maintaining the given social order for its own sake.

EXAMPLE 4: If we don't educate our children (teach our children to show respect for authority), society will fall apart.

STAGE 5: The Social Contract, Legalistic Orientation. Right action tends to be defined in terms of general individual rights and standards which have been critically examined and agreed upon by the whole society. There is a clear awareness of the relativism of personal values and opinions and a corresponding emphasis upon procedural rules for reaching consensus. Aside from what is constitutionally and democratically agreed upon, the right is a matter of personal "values" and "opinion." The result is an emphasis upon the "legal point of view," but with the possibility stressed of changing law in terms of rational considerations of social utility (rather than freezing it in terms of Stage 4, "law and order"). Outside the legal realm, free agreement and contract is the binding element of obligation. This is the "official" morality of the American government and Constitution.

EXAMPLE 5: Education is a right of every citizen, guaranteed by the Constitution, necessary for sound economy and preservation of human rights.

Table 1 (continued)

STAGE 6: The Universal-Ethical Principle Orientation. Right is defined by the decision of conscience in accord with self-chosen ethical principles appealing to logical comprehensiveness, universality and consistency. These principles are abstract and ethical (the Golden Rule), they are not concrete moral rules like the Ten Commandments. At heart, these are universal principles of justice, of the reciprocity and equality of human rights and/or respect for the dignity of human beings as individual persons.

EXAMPLE 6: Each individual has unique capabilities which deserve nurturance within the limits of effective functioning in a society which values individual contributions and varied life styles.

mine once said, "There is nothing more tragic then the teacher who has a good way with children and nothing to offer them." Schooling is a deliberate intervention by adults into the lives of students, and if there is no payoff, no goal reached, education becomes an inappropriate imposition. Furthermore, an absence of goals is an absence of expectations, and in the absence of expectations, education becomes an insult. Suggestions for developing consensus on aims may be found in Rippey (1973) and Page (1974).

Perhaps more important than goals clearly stated, are goals that are clearly understood. This means that goals may need translation, explanation and reevaluation. They should be understood by more than the persons who wrote them. As was the case with the terrible twelve, they might not have cared much for the collegiate version of their objectives, but they could tell you what the goals meant to them, and that came through talking together about goals and living in an environment which exemplified those goals.

This also means that the school must take the responsibility for more parent education in goals. It is important to check parent understanding through a continual dialogue. Can they tell you what the goals of the school are and what they mean to them? If some goals are better than others, they should know why. Only if they are clear about goals can they tell you whether these goals are evidenced in the thoughts and actions of their children. Although I am in favor of having the goals of the school written formally in terms of behavioral objectives somewhere in a form accessible to teachers, these are no substitutes for a clear picture of the school's aims embedded in the minds of parents and students, rather than in the cornerstone of the school building.

There are many models for parent education, ranging from the simpler voluntary programs offered by PTAs to the more comprehensive programs involving regular classroom meetings with children, such as those advocated by Bessel and Palomares (1970), or those in the Chicago Public Schools, Woodlawn Mental Health Center and PACE programs (Schiff, 1972). Even more ambitious, the Woodlawn Experimental Schools Project had a formalized program of training parent community organizers to take a very direct role in influencing the aims and the directions of the schools. In his report on the early years of the PACE program, Schiff states: "The real core of the program—an enduring commitment to free inquiry—became indistinguishable from a commitment to change . . . Evidence does exist that inexpensive, properly conceived and implemented programs based on a sustained commitment can work. Such evidence is in direct conflict with the published judgment of such academics as Banfield, Lowi and Moynihan, whose lack of direct, continuous involvement with the residents of such neighborhoods renders their analysis vulnerable to the criticism of ivory-towerism."

This commitment to free inquiry—problem-solving, if you will—in conjunction with education suggests a radical change in our attitudes toward school. Schools have often been considered competent arms of the state, qualified to produce good citizens and to repress vandalism, malicious mischief and unnatural acts.

The concept of school being an experiment—albeit an experiment in living and growing—is incongruous to many and abhorrent to some. The very idea of a school devoted to inquiry and learning—not having the answers to the big questions of Love and Death—sounds almost seditious.

I Don't Want My Kid
to Be a Guinea Pig

Perhaps one of the greatest protests to the concept of schooling as an experiment is that of making children guinea pigs. This is the farthest thing from my mind. School is enough of that sort of an experiment as it is. What I mean by school as an experiment goes back to Dewey (1916, 1927) and beyond. I refer to a school which exemplifies problem-solving; a school which solves problems rather than perpetuates them. In the problem-solving school, the teachers don't perform experiments on the children, they perform them on the *school*. The children perform experiments in living and learning. The school encourages and exemplifies the utilization of Dewey's four steps:

(1) concrete experience;
(2) reflective observation of problematic elements in the environment;
(3) abstract conceptualization, theorizing, hypothesis generation; and
(4) active experimentation.

In a problem-solving school, one can imagine a curriculum based on a set of intended outcomes, growing out of a set of hypotheses on reflective observation of problematic elements in the student's environment. The validity of such a program would be confirmed by careful evaluation of its outcomes. There would be a continuous reevaluation and recycling going on, and no aspect of the curriculum would be cast in concrete. Yet, at any time, no one would be in the dark about either the aims or the criteria for assessing their accomplishments. The conceptualization and testing of hypotheses would be complemented and enriched by much of what is considered traditional subject matter. New ideas and methodology would be introduced as the nature of problems demanded. The hypotheses would range from "What is it like to be an adult?" and "How can I get along better with my friends?" to "What are the problems of confining plasma in a fusion reaction?" and "What is the meaning of angle in a Behrens-Fisher distribution?" In the problem-solving environment, it would not be the child who was the guinea pig, but the world, and rather than being taught today's answers, the child would learn to formulate tomorrow's questions. Technology would have no trouble fitting into this school because technology would seldom be abused. Appropriateness would be monitored. In fact, the school would represent the best in humane technology—technology in the service of people. It would not entertain technology simply because technology was there (Rippey, 1963).

Those concerned with the possibility of children being used as the subjects for educational experiments should also consider the current system of education. Does it provide the normal guarantees provided the subject of other forms of human experimentation? When this thought first occurred to me, I was amused, but when I looked again at some of the key documents underlying the protection of human subjects, I was not amused at all. It seemed that perhaps insufficient safeguards were being given to the children in schools.

Two of the key documents on human experimentation are the Nurenberg Code and the Declaration of Helsinki. First, the Nurenberg Code (Katz, 1972).

Article one requires the informed consent of all subjects. Article two requires that the experiment should yield fruitful results for the good of society, which are not procurable by other means. Article three requires that the experiment should be based on the results of prior knowledge so that anticipated results will justify the performance of the experiment. Article four requires that the experiment be conducted so as to avoid both physical and mental suffering and injury. Sections five through seven are perhaps not so relevant to education. Article eight requires that the experiment be conducted only by qualified persons who would be bound to exercise the highest degree of skill and care through all stages of the experiment. Sections nine and ten allow for the termination of the experiment at the option of either the subject or the experimenter.

The Declaration of Helsinki reiterates these basic points. Again, the principle of informed consent (knowledge of objectives) is emphasized although proxy consent by parents is allowed. An additional point in the Helsinki Declaration is: "The investigator must respect the right of each subject (student) to safeguard his personal integrity, especially if the subject is in a dependent relationship to the investigator (teacher).

In the absence of other criteria for evaluating schooling, one could do worse than to start with these principles. Replacing the experiment with schooling, the subject by the pupil and the investigator by the teacher, the questions to be asked are: To what extent is the student informed of the aims of the schooling? To what extent does he consent? To what extent does he have the power and capability of either consent or dissent? From article two, we wonder to what extent schooling yields fruitful results for the good of society, not procurable by other means? Has this question ever been seriously tested? From article three, to what extent have the practices and procedures of schooling been validated by prior evidence? From the other articles, to what extent is suffering minimized? To what extent is schooling conducted by the most qualified, and do they in fact exercise the highest levels of skill and care? And, finally, to what extent is termination (or interruption) allowed or considered as even a valid option?

To me, the benefits of charging the school with the dominant aim of free inquiry seem much greater than the risks.

At best, such a school would perhaps fit into the utopia envisioned by Nobel prize winner Jacques Monod (Monod, 1971):

> Where then shall we find the source of truth and the moral
> inspiration for a really scientific socialist humanism, if not in the

sources of science itself, in the ethic upon which knowledge is founded, and which by free choice makes knowledge the supreme value—the measure and warrant of all other values? An ethic which bases moral responsibility upon the very freedom of that axiomatic choice ... [That ethic] prescribes institutions dedicated to the defense, the extension, the enrichment of the transcendent kingdom of ideas, of knowledge and creation—a kingdom which is within man, where progressively freed both from material constraints and from the deceitful servitudes of animism, he could at last live authentically, protected by institutions which, seeing him the subject of the kingdom, and at the same time its creator, could be designed to serve him in his unique and precious essence.

At its very worst, it would contain sufficient internal controls to self destruct in case of malfunction—something which precious few contemporary schools possess.

Some Aims Are
Better Than Others

Perhaps, by now, you have not only become convinced of the importance of clarifying the aims of schooling, but also have clarified your own set of values about schooling. Compare them with my utopia. My own preferred school would be one where children would have a variety of clear goals to work on, about two-thirds provided by the school and about a third developed through reciprocal negotiation and clarification with the teacher. In this school, the child would be able to work alone part of the time, work with other children part of the time, and play part of the time. His teachers would not be anxious about themselves or about him. Teachers would have clearly articulated expectations for him, and would make challenging though not excessively difficult demands on him; he would be encouraged and rewarded for active participation in learning activities and school life, not just for success or excellence. Special efforts would be made by teachers to make him feel safe, competent and accepted. I would like institutional expectations of the school to focus on reading with enjoyment and understanding, writing with meaning and feeling, developing technical competence on the way, but not making a fetish of producing technically correct rubbish. In arithmetic, I would like him to develop an appreciation of number and ways of expressing relationships, but would not burden him with dreary pointless and endless computation. Much of the rest, I would leave to him and the enthusiasm of his teacher. I would want the school to keep track of student performance by careful evaluation using methods in harmony with the clear and articulated aims. But, above all, the child would observe, reflect, question and test.

Should it happen that my great-grandchildren might have the privilege of attending such a simple and internally consistent school, and if, in this far off age where this fantasy might be realized, in this postulated golden age of educational maturity, some careful investigator might bring forth the crinkled pages of an ancient SAT test and administer it to this class of the year 2001, he might find that the downward trend in SAT scores had in fact reversed itself. But in such an age of enlightenment and enlightened schools, would anyone really care?

References

Bessel, H. and U. Palomares. *Methods in Human Development Theory*. San Diego: Human Development Training Institute, 1970.

Cotten, J. Theoretical Perspectives for Research on College Training: A Cognitive Viewpoint. Paper presented to the Conference on Research on College Training, Northwestern University, Evanston, Illinois, May 24-26, 1973.

Dewey, J. *Democracy and Education*. New York: Macmillan, 1916.

Dewey, J. *The Sources of a Science of Education*. New York: Liverwright, 1927.

Dreeben, R. *On What Is Learned in School*. Reading, Mass.: Addison-Wesley, 1968.

Ehrlich, V.Z. The Dimensions of Attitude Toward School of Elementary School Children in Grades 3 to 6. Unpublished Doctoral Dissertation, Columbia University, 1969.

Erikson, E. *Identity and the Life Cycle*. New York: International Universities Press, 1959.

Jackson, P. *Life in Classrooms*. New York: Holt, Rinehart and Winston, 1968.

Katz, J. *Experimentation with Human Beings*. New York: Russell Sage Foundation, 1972.

Marland, S. Reported in *Chronicle of Higher Education*, January 26, 1976.

Monod, J. *Chance and Necessity*. New York: Vintage Books, 1971.

Page, E.B. Top Down Trees of Educational Values. *Educational and Psychological Measurement*, 1974.

Rippey, R. Pineblossom High Versus the 7011. *Data Processing for Education*, April 1963, *2*(4), 1-7.

Rippey, R. *Studies in Transactional Evaluation*. Berkeley: McCutchan, 1973.

Schiff, S. Free Inquiry and the Enduring Commitment: The Woodlawn Mental Health Center, 1963-70. In S. Golann and C. Eisdorfer (Eds.) *Handbook of Community Mental Health*. New York: Appleton-Century-Crofts, 1972.

Turiel, E. Stage Transition in Moral Development. In R.M.W. Travers (Ed.) *Second Handbook of Research on Teaching*. Chicago: Rand McNally, 1973.

White, M.A. The View from the Pupil's Desk. *Urban Review*, 1968, 5-11.

11.

An Exercise in Freedom:
A Place Where Test Scores
Appear to Be Rising

David W. Champagne and
Eric J. Roberts

Introduction

There are times and places which do not follow trends. These apparent anomalies demand our attention if we are to comprehend them. Situations which resist trends we don't like are especially worthy of careful consideration. The setting which provides the information we shall discuss is not the sort of place we normally would expect to offer a strong reversal of the decade-long slide of achievement scores in American schools. *But it has.* We propose an explanation of this anomaly. We do so with the conviction that what we suggest is a responsible explanation. We know that these conclusions are—for us—inescapable. Others, yet to be offered, may be more reasonable. We don't know—for sure.

The Setting

The community served by this school is a Western Pennsylvania mill town. Like so many others scattered throughout the area, the town is surrounded by beautiful, rolling hills intertwined with river valleys. Driving through the countryside, you sometimes get a sense of how magnificent the area must have been, before.

David W. Champagne is Associate Professor of Curriculum and Instruction, University of Pittsburgh, Pennsylvania. **Eric J. Roberts** is a doctoral candidate at the University of Pittsburgh and a curriculum writer at the Learning Research and Development Center.

No one would describe the town as beautiful now. The river, while prominent, is almost totally inaccessible to the people, made remote—and undesirable—by the railroads and mills on its banks which own, use and pollute it. Up the hill, away from the closely packed first-generation streets of the old town, there are the newer, second- and third-generation streets—wider, flatter and greener.

That's where the junior and senior high schools are too. The junior high building used to house the senior high before it was outgrown. In the last year, underground mine subsidence, endemic to many areas of the state, has caused extensive damage to the building and to the athletic fields. The new senior high building is four or five years old. It is modern and comfortable, but no Taj Mahal. It will continue to meet the needs of the community, as population projections suggest a modest decline in enrollment from about 740 to about 685 tenth-, eleventh- and twelfth-grade students over the next few years.

The Data

Many of the students in this district take the Scholastic Aptitude Tests (SATs), the College Boards. The Pennsylvania Department of Education has recently begun another testing program, this one called the Educational Quality Assessment (EQA). This statewide program measures achievement as well as certain attitudinal goals of public education.

Before reporting the data from these various tests, we offer another form of data, a calendar of events which took place in this school; see Table 1. An appreciation of these data is crucial for a thorough comprehension of the tests' numbers.

Every April the SATs are given to the junior class. All students in this school are urged to take the test whether or not they have active plans to go to college.

The SAT scores are reported for the last decade in this school district; see Table 2.

Table 1

Timetable of Events in This Intervention

Fall 1971   First EQA given at senior high.

Spring 1972   EQA results returned from state department of education.

Summer 1972   EQA staff interpreted school results with district adminis-
                   trators.

Academic Year   Series of after-school meetings with faculty and adminis-
1972-73   trators explaining and examining results. Results also shared
                   with school board and community. Student and faculty
                   "rap" sessions held to discuss meanings and implications of
                   data.

Spring 1973   At the initiation of the school district's administration and
                   based on teachers' ideas, the school district wrote and was
                   funded for a three-year Title III project to attempt an
                   increase in EQA results, chiefly in the area of "Interest in
                   School."

Summer 1973   Title III workshop I. Participants: 35 volunteer faculty
                   from junior high and senior high; 25 students; 10 parents;
                   all junior- and senior-high administrators; one federal
                   projects coordinator; one school superintendent; two
                   school board members; four university consultants. (There
                   were not then, and still are not, any other supervisory or
                   curriculum personnel in the district.)

Academic Year   High-interest projects carried out. Rap groups of teachers,
1973-74   students, parents and administrators meet occasionally in
                   senior high during evenings. Consultants come to reinforce
                   faculty in Spring.

Summer 1974   Title III workshop II. Organized by school district with
                   some planning consultation with University consultants.
                   More projects planned.

Academic Year   Some projects offered again; new projects offered. Some
1974-75   rap groups talking about progress. Senior high focus of

Table 1 (continued)

	most projects. EQA administered, Spring '75, to junior and senior highs.
Summer 1975	Title III workshop III. Shorter workshop organized by district. Some reinforcement by original consultant. Continued verbal commitment to project.
Academic Year 1975-76	Reduced level of projects. Not many new ideas. District shows some apparent change back toward earlier ways of doing things in senior high. Junior high relatively inactive.
Summer 1976	End of Title III and project.

During the years when the Title III project was being implemented, the scores began to climb. The last year for which data are available show the verbal and math scores almost at the 1968 figure. The national trend during this period has been directly opposite, with a drop of more than 20 points resulting in the 1975 administration—while this district was *jumping 30 points.*

This district does maintain a modest norm-referenced testing program of its own. The data are not presented here because the tests in the past have not been given at exactly comparable times and because they have not been given using all the procedures recommended by the test designers.

Qualitative Data

The superintendent's records show that during the first two years of the Title III project (Project IDEA, "Interest Developed through Educational Awareness"), vandalism and disciplinary suspensions dropped in the senior high school. Average daily attendance increased during the academic years 1973-74 and 1974-75 over previous years.

No visible changes occurred in this school district's popula-

Table 2

SAT Scores

Year Test Given	Verbal	Math	Total	
1965	448.2	497.3	954.5	
1966	463.6	498.4	962.0	
1967	------unavailable------			
1968	430.2	474.2	904.4	
1969	412.0	470.8	882.8	
1970	428.8	466.5	895.3	
1971	429.5	468.5	895.0	
1972	423.8	468.9	892.7	
1973	374.3	442.9	817.2	
1974	409.5	462.7	872.2	First two years of Title III Project
1975	420.7	481.7	902.4	

tion pool. Few families moved into or out of the area. Employment conditions did not change. The faculty turn-over during this time included no more than a handful of positions. No administrative or central office personnel changed. There were no new curricular projects initiated other than the Title III grant. This intervention was the only one in this district at this level. The curriculum was at that time, and continues to be, a traditional, comprehensive high school program. There was *no* direct attempt to increase either verbal or math scores on the EQA or the SAT tests, in the senior high school. The Title III project focused only on increasing interest in school.

The only explanation for the very dramatic changes in both EQA scores in the two separate environments (junior and senior high schools) which makes sense to us is that they are somehow tied to the Title III Project, IDEA intervention. But the effects appear to have been opposite in the two different places! The senior high school scores increased dramatically. The junior high school scores dropped dramatically.

Project IDEA, a Three-Year
Title III Intervention Project

The ESEA Title III grant made funds available for attempts at increasing student interest in school, in both junior and senior high schools. The district's chief administrators felt that school must be a place where students feel that they are cared about and where students are interested in and value what they are learning. The administrators felt that the alternative to interested, self-motivated students was repressed students. They also felt that high student interest in school would be reflected in increased school achievement scores. With these beliefs in mind, they identified these specific goals for their proposal.

> Students shall exhibit a self-motivated curiosity about learning and show an inquisitiveness about discovery and inquiry.

> Students shall attend school more consistently as a result of more challenging and stimulating activities within the classroom and throughout the school environment.

> Students shall show a sense of belonging by greater and more frequent participation in extra-curricular activities.

> Students shall exhibit an initiative in goal-setting and success evaluation.

> Students shall display an attitude of ease and confidence in communicating with faculty, administration and peers.*

The beginning experience of Project IDEA was a three-week (four days a week, with four hours a day) summer workshop for 35 volunteer teachers (both from junior and senior high schools),

Project IDEA, Published Bulletin (Federal Projects No. 73001), Freedom Area School District, Freedom, Pennsylvania, 1974.

25 students (from both schools, and with varying levels of academic achievement and varying attitudes about school), 10 parents, all secondary school administrators, the project directors, the school superintendent and two school board members.

This workshop set the tone for the whole intervention project. Its objectives, congruent with the thrust of the total project, were:

> To have educators participate in experiences which exemplify a relationship between the learner and the teacher, developing shared responsibilities for the content and process of the learning;

> To have educators learn and practice specific skills of communication and instruction appropriate to this developing relationship;

> To have educators develop specific units of material, using these instructional techniques, and to have these techniques integrate community-related experiences with school-related experiences.

The first week of the workshop consisted entirely of communications exercises among the participants. *All* participants were on a first-name basis by the end of this time. In the second week of this workshop, all participants (teachers, students, parents, administrators and board members) received instruction in and practice at eight different types of small-group, high-interest instructional techniques. During the third week of the workshop, all participants, under the leadership of individual faculty members, designed instructional projects using one or more of these techniques. Each faculty member signed an individual contract agreeing to use that project during the 1973-74 school year. The students and parents had first to agree that these projects were worthwhile, and sounded interesting. Administrators agreed to facilitate scheduling and special arrangements for all projects.

Similar contracts were signed in the following summer's

workshop. Sixty-eight projects are described by the schools as having been carried out during the two academic years. Fifty-nine of these projects originated in the senior high school and involved all tenth-, eleventh- and twelfth-grade students at least once, although many students were involved in several. Guest speakers were invited into classes in addition to the projects. Only nine projects were reported in the junior high school. Three of these nine are described as direct skill-building activities. Faculty members were encouraged to attend conferences for their own professional growth. All of the formal faculty development experiences reported were initiated and attended by senior high school faculty.

Since there are no formal supervisory or reinforcement personnel in the district, the federal projects coordinator assumed this role. He was housed in the senior high school building. Most of his time and emphasis was in this building, focused on this population—both students and faculty.

An Analysis

Even a cursory glance at the EQA (see Table 3 and Table 4) data shows conflicting results in the two different schools. In the junior high school only two goal percentile scores are increased: those of basic skills achievement. Six goals dropped in percentile compared to the norm group. Two goals remained the same. The largest percentile drop was in Goal IV, Interest in School and Learning. The two scores on this goal dropped from the 50th percentile to the 5th percentile. The next largest drop, of 38 percentile points, was the area of Goal IX, Appreciating Human Accomplishments.

The junior high school faculty has been characterized by the administrative staff as basically conservative and highly motivated toward basic skills learning. During these two academic years they seemed to have focused their efforts in these areas. Our observation, supported by the number of projects, the numbers of students involved and the thrust of the projects, suggests that the

Table 3

Junior High School EQA Results
Scores Percentile (compared to state-wide norm group)

	EQA Goal	Test Scores Spring 1973	EQA Goals**	Test Scores Spring 1975	Percentile Change in Scores 1973-1975
I.	Self-Esteem	50	Self-Esteem	37	-13
II.	Understanding Others	18	Understanding Others	7	-11
III-V.	Basic Skills: Verbal	50	Basic Skills: Verbal	67	+17
III-M.	Basic Skills: Math	47	Basic Skills: Math	60	+13
IV.	Interest in School	50	Interest in School and Learning	5	-45
V.	Citizenship	37	Societal Responsibility	37	0
VI.	Health Habits	50	Health Habits	40	-10
VII.	Creativity	40	Creative Activities/Recognition	40	0
*VIII-A.	Vocational Attitude	77	Career Attitude (11th grade only)	--	--
*VIII-K	Vocational Knowledge	63	Career Awareness	67	--
IX.	Appreciating Human Accomplishments	45	Appreciating Human Accomplishments	7	-38
X.	Preparing for a Changing World	33	Coping with Change	23	-10

*Uninterpretable with the change in category and the collapsing of these two categories into one.

**All goals except for those noted are the same; changes seem more in titles than in substance.

Table 4

Senior High School EQA Results
Scores Percentile (compared to state-wide norm group)

	EQA Goals	Test Scores Fall 1971	EQA Goals	Test Scores Spring 1975	Percentile Change in Scores 1971-1975
I.	Self-Understanding	69	Self-Esteem	40	-29
II.	Understanding Others	14	Understanding Others	41	+27
III-V.	Basic Skills: Verbal	21	Basic Skills: Verbal	54	+33
III-M.	Basic Skills: Math	16	Basic Skills: Math	38	+22
IV.	Interest in School	8	Interest in School and Learning	56	+48
V.	Citizenship	4	Societal Responsibility	23	+19
VI.	Health Habits	3	Health and Safety Practices	39	+36
VII.	Creative Potential	54	Creative Activities	32*	?
	Creative Output	84	----------	--	--
VIII.	Vocational Development	14	Career Attitudes	31	+17
IX.	Appreciating Human Accomplishments	1	Appreciating Human Accomplishments	29	+28
X.	Preparing for a Changing World	46	Coping with Change	34	-12

*Uninterpretable with the collapsing of these two categories into one but score is definitely down.

junior high school faculty's beginning involvement in the project was small and dropped during the second year. This faculty's high interest as a group in basic skills has produced gains in these scores. We reckon the cost of these gains too high, however, if they must be achieved at the expense of students' interest in school and appreciation of human accomplishments as marked by these figures. The drop to these low levels suggests major future problems. Furthermore, we believe that if students have very low interest in school, they may seek temporary flight from their aversive atmosphere through absenteeism, cutting classes and vandalism. Later they may very likely seek permanent escape by leaving school entirely, as soon as that is legally possible for them. These data certainly do not lead us to an optimistic attitude about the likelihood of these people becoming interested, excited, self-motivated learners in the future.

Project IDEA had its real impact in the senior high school. The primary goal focus, student interest in school, showed the greatest percentile gains (+48 percent) compared with the norm population. Positive health habits and safety practices, Goal VI—within which are drug use and abuse items—increased the next greatest amount (+36 percent). If these changes represent real changes in students' attitudes, and we see no evidence to the contrary, they may be linked to more open school practices and more honest relationships with the adult models in the school. Goal IX, Appreciating Human Accomplishments, which increased by 28 percentile points, is directly related, in our minds, to interest in school.* Participation in school projects that have contact with a wide range of human achievements has directly increased interest in these accomplishments, and in the school environment which provides these projects.

The direction of the curriculum, the scope of the curriculum and the dispersion of the students within the school have remained

---

*Probably not coincidentally, these two areas were ones which dropped the greatest in the junior high school.

the same. There has been no specific effort in the senior high school which applied greater time or energy on basic skills development. On the contrary, time spent on special projects has resulted in decreased total time spent on basics (since total time in school remained the same). Yet the increases in basic skills-verbal (+33 percent) and basic skills-math (+22 percent) are even greater in this environment than in the junior high school, where specific efforts were directed at these areas. The comparatively greater increase in basic skills in the senior high school has not been at the incredible cost of dropping interest in school. On the contrary, eight of the EQA goals show strong increases.

We do not mean to ignore the two areas of the EQA where the senior high school results show a decrease. We believe our explanation of the major trends can be extended to cover these two goals. The students dropped in both Self-Esteem, Goal I, and Coping with Changes, Goal X. The same projects which brought these students into contact with a broader spectrum of the world and its experiences brought the students a more realistic view of themselves in relation to that world. Coming out of a cocoon is not necessarily an easy experience, even if it eventually produces beautiful butterflies. Realization of this larger world may have been part of a motivation for greater achievements in academic areas.

The increase in SAT scores during the first two years of the Title III project may be an accidental correlation with the EQA results. An accident of this magnitude seems to be stretching coincidence a long way, however.

Conclusions

We have suggested in our analysis that increasing student interest in school seems to be the most likely explanation for increases in student achievement scores on norm-referenced tests, even when no other portions of the curriculum are changed in noticeable ways. We suggest that increasing time and effort directly on basic skills can lead to some increases in skill learning, but may also result in other, very undesirable effects on student interests. These undesirable effects may even be more significant in the long run than the increases in skills learning. For example, what would happen if in an attempt to increase basic skills scores;

the schools began to use more traditional teaching methods, or

the schools dropped many of the high-interest activities, or

the schools began to institute more traditional rules, perceived by the students as negative, repressive and less trusting of them?

It's not unlikely that these things could happen; none of the above possibilities represents an impossible reactionary swing of the pendulum away from freedom. Teachers can get tired. Teachers and administrators can feel frustration at the loss of traditional controls. And parents can feel moved to exert pressures against the confusion that results when their children are not supplied the strictures that have for so long characterized schooling. But if those things happen, we predict that there will be trouble. In an area as fragile as the developing relationships of Project IDEA, the adverse effects would be visible almost immediately. Vandalism and discipline problems would edge back up. Attendance figures would slide back down. Less open and honest communications would take place. The social distance between learner and learner's helper (i.e., teacher) would widen. And those are only some of the symptoms. If these few symptoms resulted from a drop in student interest in school, then a secondary effect would be a drop in achievement test scores. Appearance of disciplinary problems in any school environment is a signal of more trouble coming.

That's what would happen IF the changes we supposed take place. We hope they don't. They don't need to.

Is it really possible to change the outcomes of a school this much, this rapidly? Can we really produce the kinds of outcomes we desire by manipulating an environment for students, by establishing more real, free relationships among students and faculty? Does a small increment of caring and trust really matter this much? Do we really have data that backs our deepest beliefs? Can we now tell the "Back to Basics" bunch why they are wrong—with more ammunition than our empassioned convictions? Can we afford to work this hard and this much with our schools, or can we not afford not to?

Obviously, we have to see this kind of effect in a lot more places, under much more controlled conditions, before we can jump off this enormous conceptual cliff. But what we have here shown ourselves is that we are already at the edge of that leap.

Of course we're prejudiced; we want to believe in this. We have wanted to so believe even before we found this data. But we now believe that these conclusions are based on more than emotional inclinations. And we are pleased to have seen this exercise in freedom.

12.

If Reading Scores Are Irrelevant, Do We Have Anything Better?

Henry Acland

There are three things we want to know about the reading score decline: Is it real? If so, what caused it? Then, what can be done about it? While logically it does not make sense to deal with the third question without having answered the first and second, I suspect the people who run schools are already responding in various ways to the perceived decline in test scores. One of these responses concerns me here; the adoption of different kinds of tests to assess educational performance. I am talking about tests of functional literacy which emphasize real-life skills rather than the problems contrived by the makers of standardized tests. These tests, which are also called tests of "adult literacy," "functional literacy" or "coping and survival skills," are becoming increasingly popular.* Clearly their use reflects dissatisfaction with traditional standardized tests. Perhaps the main complaint is that standardized tests do not measure what schools are trying to teach. Competency tests have a satisfying tangibility which seems to meet this deficiency. Besides, the new tests have a very obvious

---

*Five states now have legislation, passed or pending, which would require students to pass competency tests at some point in their educational career, most usually upon graduation from high school (information from the Education Commission of the States).

Henry Acland is Assistant Professor, School of Education, University of Southern California, Los Angeles.

credibility; teachers can readily demonstrate the importance of the types of knowledge that the tests measure, and this is one basis on which they can respond to the pressures of accountability.)

In this article I concentrate most of my attention on a sophisticated competency test: the Adult Performance Level Functional Literacy Test (Northcutt, 1975). My aim is to explore the credibility of this test as a device for differentiating the competent from the incompetent. The argument is simple: any test of competency assumes we can judge what it takes to get by, and having judged it, we can measure it. To measure this capacity requires two further steps. The first involves identification of problems which *all* people need to solve in their everyday lives. The second involves defining the *right and wrong* ways of solving these universal problems. In other words, for a test to be generally useful we need to select problems which everyone must deal with and then decide on the best way those problems can be solved. To put this the other way around, to the degree that people do not contend with the same problems and to the degree they have viable, but unorthodox, ways of dealing with those problems they do have in common—to that degree we must acknowledge the difficulty, perhaps the impossibility, of constructing a test of competence.

I shall make two main points. First, people do not face the same problems. Specifically, rich people's problems are not poor people's problems, and vice versa. Therefore, the skills that it takes to get by in one social group are different from those required in another. Second, there is a variety of ways of solving a problem. In important instances it is impossible to define "right" and "wrong" ways of dealing with a situation. Although these points may seem elementary, they must be attended to, because they undercut the credibility of the tests. If these tests have serious shortcomings, we should be aware of them, and consider the implications of acting as if we have credible ways of assessing competency.

The Adult Performance Level
Functional Literacy Test (APL)

The APL is not chosen because it is poorly designed; just the opposite. It is better researched and more carefully thought out than other competency tests I have seen. And if the points made here seem critical, it must be remembered that the art of composing such tests is likely to develop considerably in the future. The APL was one of the first attempts to operationalize a measure of competency. If future tests develop with somewhat different emphases, they will undoubtedly build on the obvious strengths of the APL. One further point: my comments on the APL can most likely be generalized to other tests, too. The APL is used here to supply examples; it is not being singled out for special attention.

APL items were grouped in four categories: consumer economics, occupational knowledge, community resources and health, and government and law. The test requires the respondent to give both written and oral answers to questions presented in written form, often with additional material like forms, pictures or maps which are essential to defining the task. The most recent 42-item version of the APL was derived from a large pool of trial items, and selection was based on the observed correlations between items and measures of adult success: income, occupational status and years of education. This method goes some way to establishing the validity of the APL, though no causal relationship is implied between people's competence assessed by the test and their rating on the adult success measures. The testmakers' use of the test scores suggests they have confidence in the validity of the test, for they divide the sample into three groups: proficient adults (46 percent of the total sample), functional adults (34 percent) and adults who function with difficulty (20 percent). This indicates the test is a trusted instrument. The Associated Press version of the results began: "more than 23 million American adults, one in every five, lack the basic know-how to function effectively in society. . . ."

Do People Face
the Same Problems?

I suggested the measurement of competency must be done using problems which everyone faces in their lives. I shall use three examples to show how hard it may be to find such universal problems.

Using Airlines

People were asked to use an airline schedule to select a flight such that they could make an appointment in another city at a specified time; 30 percent failed to get the right flight. The airline schedule was chosen to represent others; bus, train and subway schedules. The testmakers took the view that if you could use the airline timetable correctly, you possessed a skill of general applicability. But the case can be made that there are skills which apply to checking airline schedules which are not necessary for other tasks. In that case it is pertinent to ask how many people use airlines. In September, 1974 only one person in two (55 percent) had *ever* flown (Gallup, 1974). This makes the "bad" result look a lot less depressing; it now seems to reflect differences in the tasks people face rather than differences in their problem-solving skills. The global figure can be broken out to reveal much more. In Table 1, I have divided the APL sample by race and by income, and compared the results of this item to the proportion of people in the same categories who have ever flown.

The numbers suggest the difficulty of deciding if the APL results demonstrate level of incompetence or merely the effects of differences in problems people cope with and solve in their daily lives. Blacks use airlines less than whites; fewer of them answer the question correctly. One reaction might be they are prevented from using the airlines just because they cannot do things like following schedules. But this idea doesn't stand up too well if one examines the results by income group. This shows that a considerably higher proportion of poor people were successful on this item (53 percent) than had actually used an airline (35 percent). By

Table 1

		Percent ever flown, 1974 Source: Gallup, 1974	Percent correctly selecting flight on APL
RACE	Black	39	51
	White	57	72
FAMILY **INCOME**	Under 3,000	32) 35	53
	3,000-4,999	37)	
	5,000-6,999	48	66
	7,000-9,999	48	66
	10,000-14,999	56	73
	15,000+	75	78

contrast, about the same proportion of the most affluent group both uses airlines and gets the right answer. Schedule-reading talents do not seem likely to account for the lower use of airlines among poor people.

One further cause for concern about this item is that an amazing 22 percent of the most affluent group fail the item. Does this mean that in real-life they are failing to make their appointments? Casual observation of airport concourses does not suggest a widespread problem. Businessmen are not found there scratching their puzzled heads figuring out schedules; rather, they seem to know where they are going so well they look like they run on wheels. To me this suggests that the schedule problem cannot be a necessary real-life skill for this group, either. After all, a lot of these people have a secretary or travel agent to solve their scheduling problems for them.

Problems Connected with Driving

If there is one competency that looks like a survival skill in America, it must be driving ability. After all, driving is so important that high school graduation requirements frequently include driver education. Besides, everyone seems to drive to work, and we all know that the public transportation systems for the most part play little part in the business of getting around. It is logical then to include items which require familiarity with maps and recognition of terms dealing with traffic. The APL map question asked for the identification of a town at which a change would be made from one highway to another on a specific journey. This was failed by 14 percent of the APL sample. On another question, 30 percent failed to identify what it meant to have the "right of way" in traffic.

As before, these questions assume that everyone needs these skills. One check on this is to look at the distribution of car ownership; in 1973 one household in six (16 percent) did not have a car (Stucker and Kirkwood, in press). Ownership breaks out by race and income as shown in Table 2.

Here we have presumptive evidence that car ownership determines your ability to answer the APL questions, though a better check on this would be to correlate test score and ownership for the same sample. If that supported my contention, it would imply that people generally have the skills they need for the problems they face. Then it would be less reasonable to interpret the failure of low income groups relative to the higher ones as a demonstration of incompetence. The table reveals something surprising. The lowest income group's performance on the APL is consonant with the frequency of car ownership in this group. But the most affluent group does much worse than you might expect, given the fact that almost all of these families own cars. In particular, I note that while just about all families with incomes over $15,000 own a car, only eight in 10 (81 percent) can answer the "right of way" question correctly. Does this mean there is a serious problem that schools with more affluent student populations should remedy? Similarly, it looks as if whites are a good deal less competent than blacks. For while nine in 10 white families own cars, only seven in 10 give the correct response to the

Table 2

	Percent of families owning at least one car, 1971 SOURCE: Mandell, et al., 1973	Percent of households owning at least one car, 1973 SOURCE: Stucker and Kirkwood	Percent correct on APL map item	Percent correct on APL "right of way" item
RACE				
Black	53		62	51
White	86		89	73

FAMILY INCOME

Percent of families owning at least one car, 1971		Percent of households owning at least one car, 1973		Percent correct on APL map item		Percent correct on APL "right of way" item
Under 5,000	54	Under 5,000	56	Under 5,000	72	57
5,000-7,499	87	5,000-8,999	72	5,000-6,999	84	65
7,500-9,999	89			7,000-9,999	85	69
10,000-14,999	95	9,000-15,999	95	10,000-14,999	88	73
15,000 +	97	16,000 +	99	15,000 +	94	81

"right of way" question. For blacks there is much better correspondence; about half own cars (53 percent) and about half (51 percent) get the item right.

Bank Account Problems

A final example is concerned with people's ability to deal with banks. One APL question asks people to fill in a check for a specified amount, the other for the completion of a deposit slip. As before, these are real-life problems only for people who have banking accounts; and though it may be forgotten, a lot of people prefer to keep their money in the teapot. The table compares the percentage of people with checking accounts and the percentage answering these two items correctly. Though the information on ownership of checking accounts is seriously out of date, the trend in ownership is upward—so these figures can be regarded as conservative estimates. See Table 3.

Again, the main problem these test results expose is for the more affluent group. Look at families with incomes over $15,000. There, nine in 10 (86 percent) have checking accounts but only seven in 10 (67 percent) can fill out a deposit slip correctly. The idea that one person in three in this income bracket cannot complete a deposit slip strains the imagination. But if we trust it as accurate and valid, then we might surmise that schools with high concentrations of children from relatively affluent homes have an important task ahead of them in providing remedial education to compensate for these deficiencies. For, by comparison, the schools attended by children of poorer parents appear to be doing a better job in preparing young adults in a way which is consistent with their future needs, since we see that about the same proportions of the lowest income group both own checking accounts and are able to fill in deposit slips.

Alternative Ways of
Solving Problems

Competency tests, like standardized tests, place strict con-

Table 3

	Percent owning a checking account, 1970 SOURCE: Katona *et al.*, 1971	Percent able to write words indicating sum of money on check	Percent able to fill in deposit slip correctly
FAMILY INCOME			
Under 3,000	44)	75	45
3,000-4,999	51) 46		
5,000-7,499	62	86	55
7,500-9,999	69	85	53
10,000-14,999	81	92	66
15,000 +	86	96	67

straints on the persons completing them. One constraint is that they must offer their solutions orally or in writing. This emphasis is ironic given the intention of measuring "real-life" skills, since it implies that most problems people face have to be dealt with by these means. The more important constraint is that the test makes no allowance for the expression of unorthodox solutions.

A straightforward example illustrates the point. An APL item asks people to evaluate the best buy in breakfast cereals. Information is given on the weight and price of three different products, and the object is to pick the one which is cheapest per unit weight. Undoubtedly, this measures a useful skill which enables people to spend their money wisely. But there is another way of getting the information you need to get the best buys, and you do not need long division to get it. Products are now unit priced in most supermarkets. Since a majority of the sample got this item right (74 percent) we might conclude that the issue of alternative solutions is moot.

Another item asks for a precise definition of normal human body temperature. Again, this is a useful piece of information, but it is not one that you have to carry in your head, since every thermometer *shows* the normal point. Therefore, while 27 percent of the population fails on this item, we cannot claim the same percentage would fail if we allowed them any method they chose of supplying the answer. What if people don't have thermometers? Then, presumably, the relevance of this piece of information is more questionable.

The same general point should be born in mind when considering the high proportion of people who make errors on the APL items dealing with the IRS income tax return. A partially complete Form 1040 is presented, and the missing information has to be supplied. One item requires the person to use a table to find the appropriate tax for a specified taxable income. Only 39 percent of the population got this right, which suggests that 61 percent of income tax returns might have this kind of error. But this does not check out; information obtained from the IRS shows the fraction of errors on the 1040 is much lower, around six percent of individual returns have an arithmetic error of *any* kind (note, all are now checked for these errors). The reason that the APL results are much more discouraging is evident; in real-life people get help. In fact, about half the individual returns are signed on the preparer's line, while a special survey undertaken for the IRS shows another 10-15 percent got assistance and did not report it. So at least 60 percent of all returns are made with some kind of help.

Yet there may be some situations where alternative solutions are effectively ruled out. One instance is the driver's license application, which would seem to require specific kinds of skills, reading and checking, and particular kinds of knowledge about the motor vehicle code. Yet in California, as one example, there are special provisions for people who cannot read and write. At present the questions are asked orally, and the test taker has to indicate the answer with paper and pencil. However, if this proves too difficult, answers can be given in interview session. This procedure is currently being reviewed and modified to further reduce the need for literacy skills.

Summary

I have made two points. First, there is suggestive evidence that different kinds of people have to cope with different kinds of problems. Therefore, "failure" measured on these competency tests may not mean people are stymied by their lack of coping skills; rather, it may only show that they lack skills which they do not really need. Second, different people probably have a variety of ways of dealing with the same problem, some conventional, some unconventional. These unorthodox ways of coping may be less efficient, but that issue should not be prejudged.

Implications

What happens if these tests, flawed or not, are widely adopted? Some have argued that competency tests, and the move to accountability they reflect, are going to revolutionize American schools (Spady, 1975). While it would be a mistake to under-emphasize the political ends served by competency testing, I would predict less colorful consequences. My prediction is that teachers will respond to proficiency tests for high school graduation by teaching a dreary list of skills in areas such as form-filling, letter-writing and marketing. For students these will appear as another senseless school ritual. Teachers will tend to find it demeaning and within four years will use their bargaining power to eliminate it.

Aside from this, we can expect to see efforts to develop new and better competency tests. Could they be improved? It follows from what I have said that they can only be improved if two assumptions are thoroughly tested. We need to find out if people do have problems in common and, to the extent they do, whether they need to solve problems in the same way. To find out would require open-ended and informal interviewing of people in their everyday lives, supplemented by observation. This information could lead in three directions.

First, we might find that people really do have different problems and different ways of solving the same problems. My inference would be that we could not then develop a competency test of general applicability. Possibly, we could develop different tests for different groups, but the implications of, say, a poor-person competency test and a rich-person competency test should be carefully weighed before entering this area.

Second, we might find that people actually do have common problems and need the same skills to solve them. That route would probably require relatively minor modifications in existing tests; for example, selecting new items and reorganizing format.

The third outcome would be quite different; the information gathered from people about their real-life problems could be used to understand and then change the barriers and snares that people face in their everyday lives. At least some of these problems are the creatures of institutions: the language of tax forms, the procedural difficulties of scholarship application or the problems of comprehending the effects of medication. If we knew how people face and deal with these difficulties, we might see ways of reducing them. Tests like the APL emphasize individuals' more or less successful adjustment to society. By contrast we could concentrate on removing society's barriers to participation. This approach has the virtue of directness. It also should succeed. As an outsider one must be impressed by the fact that it is easy to find one's way around America, literally in the physical sense, but also socially. People do not leave you in doubt, the signs are easily read. This enthusiasm for plain speaking, for laying out directions, would fit with a ready acceptance of efforts to simplify or eliminate the barriers I am talking about. America could be a society where you do not have to be "competent" to participate.

References

Gallup Organization: The Incidence of Air Travel Among the General Public. Survey conducted for the Air Transport Association of America, 1974.

Katona, G., L. Mandell and J. Schmiedeskamp. *1970 Survey of Consumer*

Finances. Survey Research Center, Institute for Social Research, University of Michigan, Ann Arbor, 1971.

Mandell, L., G. Katona, J. Morgan and J. Schmiedeskamp. *Surveys of Consumers 1971-72.* Survey Research Center, Institute for Social Research, University of Michigan, Ann Arbor, 1973.

Northcutt, N. *Adult Functional Competency: A Summary.* Industrial and Business Training Bureau, Division of Extension, University of Texas at Austin, 1975.

Spady, W. Competency Based Education as a Framework for Analyzing School Reform. *Proceedings of the Third Annual Conference of the Sociology of Education Association,* 1975.

Stucker, J. and T. Kirkwood. *The Distributional Implications of Federal Policies for Reducing Gasoline Consumption* (R-1842-NSF/FEA). Rand Corporation, Santa Monica, California (in press).

13.

The Writing Skills Decline:
So What?

Gabriel Della-Piana, Lee Odell,
Charles Cooper and George Endo

Over the past decade writing skills as assessed by standardized tests appear to have declined. We provide data illustrative of the decline, analyze the probable causes, and discuss implications for program and test development.

Della-Piana and Endo are jointly responsible for the first and last sections of the report, in which some data on decline are presented, the probable causes analyzed and implications for test and program development hinted at. These sections are approached from the perspective of evaluation and the technology of education. Odell and Cooper are jointly responsible for the middle section of the article. They approach their task from the perspective of the field of English rhetoric and the training of teachers of English. Their attention is focused on an analysis of three tests of writing skills.

Data on the Writing Skills Decline

The data presented here are illustrative of what appears to be convincing evidence of a real decline in writing skills as currently assessed by standardized tests.

Gabriel Della-Piana is Director and George Endo is Research Associate, Bureau of Educational Research, University of Utah, Salt Lake City. Lee Odell and Charles Cooper are Professors, Department of Instruction, State University of New York at Buffalo.

Munday (1976) presented the major findings of the achievements of Iowa students in grades 3 to 8 and from 1955 to 1975 as measured by the Iowa Tests of Basic Skills (ITBS). Approximately 50,000 students are assessed yearly as part of the statewide Iowa testing program. The ITBS contains a language skills section which yields a total language score and separate subscores for spelling, capitalization, punctuation and usage. From 1955 to 1965, Iowa students in each grade showed improvement in all the tested areas of language skills. Declining test scores on all subtests occurred during the 1965-1970 interval, with an even more substantial drop between the 1970-1975 period. The amount of loss was positively associated with higher grade levels.

During the 1965-70 interval, children in grades 3 and 4 exhibited their greatest loss in capitalization and punctuation. Fifth grade children during the same interval showed the largest decline in capitalization and word usage. However, through grades 6-8 word usage skills dropped considerably more than other language skills. During the 1970-75 interval, children of all grades demonstrated the greatest loss in capitalization and punctuation skills.

According to Munday, the decline in language skills of Iowa pupils is not unlike those exhibited by students nationwide, although the national decline is neither as dramatic nor consistent as is found in Iowa. He further indicated that similar patterns of decline are noted in Canadian elementary school children.

Achievement scores of high school students in Minnesota and Iowa as measured by the Minnesota Scholastic Aptitude Test (MSAT) and the Iowa Tests of Educational Development (ITED) were also summarized by Munday. While no specific data on the MSAT for language skills were given, a genuine decline of composite scores was observed. The English section of the ITED, reportedly a measure of correctness and appropriateness of expression, indicates a general downward trend from 1965 to 1974 for Iowa students in the 9th, 10th, 11th and 12th grades.

Analyses of ACT English scores for male and female

college-bound and college-enrolled students revealed a general decline for both groups (Ferguson and Maxey, 1976). While the drop in English for both groups is of a larger magnitude for females than for males, the females still retained a higher mean score.

A decade of decline has also been noted on the Scholastic Aptitude Test (SAT). According to the *College Board News* (January, 1976), the 1975 SAT scores of high school graduates revealed the largest drop (10 points on the verbal part and eight points on the mathematical part) in any single year. Females showed a substantial decline on the verbal part, more so than males, and even fell below the male average (Harnischfeger and Wiley, 1976).

In sum, a variety of standardized test results has shown a general decline in language skills of elementary, secondary, college-bound and college-enrolled students. Many investigators (e.g., Ferguson and Maxey, 1976; Harnischfeger and Wiley, 1976; Munday, 1976) have concluded that the decline is widespread, pervasive and real. Many explanations have been offered for the decline (see below) and by and large a multiple causation explanation appears most plausible.

But what do declines in achievement scores for language skills mean? With respect to grades, the predictive validity coefficient between ACT test scores and high school and college grades has *not* varied to any great extent (Munday, 1976).

With respect to actual writing skills, some of the answer may come from a study conducted by the National Assessment of Educational Progress (NAEP). The NAEP Study of Writing Mechanics (1969-1974) indicates a general decline in the quality of composition produced by 17- and 13-year-old students.

For the 17-year-olds, the study found the mean holistic score (based on general impression of the reader's response to the whole essay and scored from 1 to 10) declined significantly. There were a few more good writers than in 1969, but a higher proportion of poor writers than in the same year. While writing mechanics (e.g., punctuation, spelling, capitalization) were reported as adequate, the findings revealed significant increases in awkwardness, run-on sentences and reduced coherence.

The 13-year-old students also exhibited a significant decline in composition quality from 1969-74 as determined by the holistic scoring system. The proportion of good writers also diminished significantly among this age group between 1969-74. In general, the average essay is shorter and contains simpler vocabulary, with an increase in run-on sentences, awkwardness and rambling prose, according to NAEP.

The nine-year-olds' composition reportedly showed some improvement between 1970-1974. In general, the typical essay shows the nine-year-old to be somewhat more sophisticated in composing. The essays are relatively free of run-on sentences and mechanical problems.

Across the three age groups, females produced higher quality essays than males. However, both groups showed a downward trend in over-all composition quality.

It is of some interest that while writing mechanics have declined markedly and consistently for Iowa pupils, according to the ITBS, the results of the NAEP for all three age groups revealed little or no problems with writing mechanics.

The assessment of writing skills in the National Assessment of Educational Progress is not without its critics. The early reports have been criticized on the basis of not getting at revision processes and not providing the kind of stimulus to writing or clarity with respect to audience that would make the assessment more consonant with how one actually writes (Maxwell, 1973; Slotnick, 1973). The inclusion of rewriting is promised for later versions of the tests (NAEP, 1975) and other changes are expected.

The SAT English test similarly has been criticized on the basis of *what* is assessed and how the data will presumably be used (Daniels, 1974). In the next section of this article Odell and Cooper criticize standardized tests of writing skills, focusing attention on three tests. Their concern is with *what* is measured and its general lack of correspondence with current theories of rhetoric and lack of validity with respect to some intended uses of the tests.

An Analysis of Three Tests of Writing Skills

Reports of students' declining scores on standardized tests of writing give rise to a number of questions: Why can't Johnny write? What's the matter with our schools (or with home environments or with our media-oriented society in general)? Why aren't teachers doing something about writing problems students appear to be having? Is there anything teachers *can* do about these problems? Any of these questions can generate a good deal of heat at school board and PTA meetings. But this heat is not accompanied by a proportionate amount of light. Emotions are raised, conflicting positions are taken and the whole issue of students' writing ability (or lack thereof) becomes clouded.

Some confusion is, perhaps, inevitable; certainly the issue is a complex one. But, we suggest, much of the confusion, much of the cloudiness, is caused not by the issue itself but by the questions people are asking about the issue. For example, all of the questions we mentioned above seem very misleading; all of them assume that we do, in fact, have valid, useful information about students' writing ability. But before we can make such an assumption, we need to ask somewhat different questions, questions that focus not on students' writing ability but on the means by which we gain information about their writing ability. We need, in short, to examine the examinations. Specifically, we need to think about the standardized multiple choice tests that are annually given to hundreds of thousands of students.

In this article we examine in some detail three well-established and widely used standardized tests of writing: McGraw-Hill Basic Skills System Writing Test—MHBSS (Raygor, 1970); Sequential Tests of Educational Progress: Writing—STEPW (Educational

Testing Service, 1957); and Missouri College English Test—MCET (Callis and Johnson, 1965). Other tests are, of course, also widely used. The selection of these tests is based on representativeness of the kind of approaches being used for assessment of writing skills in standardized tests. We will examine them in the context of these questions:

- Do they measure what they *say* they measure?
- Do they measure what they *should* measure?
- Do they provide results useful for diagnosis and teaching?
- Must we use them in order to obtain reliable ratings or descriptions of writing performance?

Our thesis is that standardized tests of writing often do not measure what they say they measure, always fail to measure what they should measure, and consequently provide us with little or no useful information either to guide teaching or to permit us to conclude confidently that school and college students are writing worse than they used to. We will argue further that there are other ways to obtain comprehensive and reliable descriptions of writing performance.

Do Standardized Tests Measure
What They Say They Measure?

McGraw-Hill Basic Skills System Writing Test. The MHBSS *Examiner's Manual* claims that the test "measures the student's skills in written composition." The general introduction to the test itself assures students that "the test will measure your ability to write correctly and effectively." Introductions to each of the three main sections of the test establish more restricted goals. The first section sets out to examine students' "ability to recognize errors in capitalization, punctuation and grammar." The second part is intended to measure students' ability to recognize sentence types, grammatically correct sentences and parallel construction within a sentence. . . [and to] choose an appropriate word to connect sentences to form an effective paragraph. The final part of the test is designed to determine students' "ability to construct effective paragraphs." As we shall show in a subsequent section of this article, these three abilities are not the only—or even the most important—skills one needs in writing. Even if the test measured these skills adequately, it still could not provide a complete picture of one's "skills in written composition." Our immediate concern is to raise questions about the test's ability to achieve even the very limited objectives to which we have just referred.

The test does appear to accomplish its first objective. Items in Part I do ask students to identify errors in capitalization, etc. Parts II and III, however, seem less successful. Items in each of these parts imply a definition of the phrases "appropriate word" and "effective paragraph": an appropriate transitional word is one that specifies unambiguously the logical or temporal relation between two sentences; similarly, an "effective paragraph" is one in which logical and temporal relations are made explicit. We agree that clarity and explicitness are, in fact, features of some "effective" paragraphs. We can think of instances in which a writer must be able to choose words that make logical and temporal relationships very explicit. But we can also think of instances in which the ability to create an effective paragraph depends on the ability to make different kinds of choices. Consider, for example, the following paragraphs from the MHBSS *Examiner's Manual*. The authors of the manual are attempting to show that the "Writing Test" has content validity.

> The universe from which the sample of items was selected for inclusion in the *MHBSS Writing Test* may well be defined as the content of the following three texts which were developed by Learning Technology Incorporated for the *McGraw-Hill Basic Skills System: Writing Skills I, Writing Skills II*, and *Paragraph Patterns*.
>
> The item specifications, prepared to reflect the relative emphasis of the various topics in these books, are listed in Table I on Page 8.
>
> After studying the content of these books, CTB/McGraw-Hill staff members prepared test items to fill these specifications.

> Every effort was made to prepare items that are answerable by
> those students who have learned rules and techniques for good
> writing, whether or not they had studied these books.

For someone well-versed in rhetorical theory, these paragraphs raise—but fail to answer—a number of important questions.
Before the test makers read the textbooks, did they examine
recent work in rhetorical theory? Did they attempt to assure
themselves that the texts were consistent with rhetorical theory
and research in composing? If not, why not? Surely any test of
writing should reflect our best understanding of the nature and
process of composing. If test makers did subject the texts to a
careful theory-based analysis, what rhetorical theory did they use
to guide their analysis? Why did they choose Theory A rather than
Theory B? Were the assumptions underlying the texts consistent
with rhetorical theory and research?

People who are seriously interested in these questions would
find it difficult to argue that the paragraphs cited above are an
effective statement about the content validity of MHBSS. The lack
of information about certain logical and temporal relationships
makes the paragraphs unpersuasive and uninformative to someone
who has a good background in rhetoric and composition. But let's
assume that the paragraphs were not written to inform or persuade
a rhetorician. Let's assume that they were written to give a brief
bit of background information to someone who knows more
about psychometrics than about rhetorical theory. For this
purpose, for this audience, the paragraphs are doubly "effective."
They serve what we assume was their intended function. Moreover, they help us explain why we question the ability of the
McGraw-Hill test to do all it claims. The test measures students'
ability to make only one kind of choice (the selection of words
and organizational patterns that make temporal and logical
relations explicit). It fails to measure students' ability to make
other kinds of choices (e.g., those based on one's sense of audience
and purpose) that writers frequently have to make in order to
compose effective paragraphs, i.e., paragraphs that do in fact

accomplish what the writer wishes to accomplish. This failure makes the answer to our original question equivocal, at best. If we accept the test's extremely restricted definition of *effective*, then we may say *Yes*, the test measures what it claims to measure. But if we insist that the definition of *effective* has to be consistent with the sort of rhetorical strategy found in the test *Manual*, then the answer has to be *No*.

Sequential Tests of Educational Progress: Writing. As does the MHBSS, the STEPW seeks to measure students' ability to organize writing and to observe certain conventions of standard written English. But the STEPW tries to go beyond this limited aim and "measure comprehensively the full range of skills involved in good writing." To this end, the tests contain items dealing with "critical thinking," "effectiveness" and "appropriateness" as well as items dealing with organization and correctness of usage. Further, items in the test not only ask a student to identify problems in a written passage but also to choose a version of the passage that solves the problems the student has identified. As the *Manual* notes, "Ability to identify errors or weaknesses in writing is not necessarily indicative of a student's ability to produce writing that is free of the same errors or weaknesses."

In its aims and procedures, the STEPW is one of the more sophisticated tests available. For all its sophistication, however, we are not persuaded that this test actually measures students' ability to "produce writing" that has the qualities mentioned above. For one thing, the test provides students with a completed piece of writing and, at specified points, asks students to choose the best of several alternative words, phrases or sentences. Occasionally, students do, in fact, have to do this in their own writing. Confronted with a completed draft of their writing, students come up with two or three versions of a passage and have to decide which version is the most clearly reasoned, the most effective, the most appropriate. But often—at least for high school and college students with whom we have worked—students' main problem is not one of choosing from existing alternatives but rather one of generating alternatives from which to choose. We can't be sure we have an accurate measure of students' ability to "produce writing" until we know whether they can create their own choices as well as choose from among alternatives someone else has created. Results of the STEPW do not let us determine whether students have the ability to create alternatives and make appropriate choices from among alternatives they themselves have created.

A second and more restricted problem arises from the STEPW's claim (under the heading "Appropriateness") that it measures students' ability to choose "a level of usage suitable to purpose and reader; i.e., using the right 'tone' and appropriate diction and employing tact where desirable." Form IB of the STEPW contains a number of items in which students are asked to make a value judgment, i.e., to choose the "best," the most "effective," the most "appropriate" version of a given passage. In all but *one* of the items, *best, appropriate* and *effective* appear to mean least ambiguous, most concise, most in keeping with the conventions of standard written English. Granted, these are important considerations in choosing an appropriate word or phrase. But they are by no means the only considerations. The following passage, which appeared on the cover of the Fall, 1971 "Price List Bulletin" of Educational Testing Service, will help explain our point.

> The prices listed herein conform with the provisions of the Executive Order stabilizing prices, wages and rents announced on August 15, 1971, and subsequent implementing orders and directives. Planned price adjustments for 1971-72 have been temporarily suspended.

Price adjustments, the passage says. Not *price changes* and not (heaven forbid) *price increases*. The choice of *adjustments* seems entirely appropriate. Not because the term is more concise or more correct than *changes* or *increases*. And certainly not because it is less ambiguous. (If anything, adjustments is slightly less clear than *increases*; it allows two possibilities [increasing and decreasing] whereas only one action is likely.) The choice of *adjustments* seems appropriate because it maintains the rather dignified tone characteristic of much of the material ETS publishes. It enables ETS to discuss an economic fact of life without resorting to the language of used car salesmen. Since the term has positive connotations (when something is "adjusted" it is usually set right, put in proper working order) it seems less likely to offend one who reads the price list.

The sort of choice reflected in *price adjustments* is important and rather complicated. Success or failure in writing often hinges on one's ability to make just this sort of choice, yet often there are no clear guidelines to help us make this choice. Frequently, criteria such as correctness, conciseness and clarity are not sufficient. We have to decide what we shall say on the basis of our sense of purpose in writing and our understanding of our relation to our audience. The STEPW rarely asks students to make this sort of choice. Consequently, it can give only a limited understanding of their ability to make "appropriate" choices.

Missouri College English Test. The *Manual* for the MCET says that the test is "generally concerned with the mechanics and effectiveness of written expression" and that the test is "designed to yield dependable data with regard to the level of student achievement in these aspects of writing proficiency." As in the MHBSS *mechanics* items in the MCET are limited to editorial matters of consistent capitalization and punctuation and correct usage, with some spelling items added in the MCET. The test does appear to measure control of those editorial matters. The measures of *effectiveness of written expression* are more problematic, however. We have the same reservations about the *effectiveness* claim in the MCET that we have for similar claims in the MHBSS and the STEPW. Part II of the test asks students to choose the best of four sentence-length expressions of an idea. Part III asks them to place the scrambled sentences of a paragraph in the best possible order. Besides being a reading task rather than a writing task, these parts of MCET are just too limited. They do not even approach the basic skill of conceiving and planning a whole piece of writing containing several paragraphs and then generating the information and ideas to achieve it.

Even if we lower our sights to measuring the students' ability to write a good sentence and a good paragraph, the MCET cannot help us. The sentence items are presented rhetorically; that is, they do not appear in context as sentences always do. Therefore, judgments about *effectiveness* are strained and unnatural. On Form A the choices struck us as either over-obvious or completely ambiguous. In several cases most or all of the choices are correct, and so the choice of *effective* is somewhat baffling.

Do Standardized Tests Measure
All That They Should Measure?

For all of the tests we've discussed thus far (indeed, for all of the tests we've ever examined) the answer has to be an emphatic *No.* They do not measure the full range of activities that are essential to effective writing. The multiple choice tests we've examined simply ask students to examine a written passage and make the relatively minor alterations that will transform the passage into an acceptable finished draft. Obviously, these editorial alterations are an important part of the composing process. But it is equally obvious to people who write a lot that the writing process does not begin with the editing of a draft. No one starts to write with a page full of words and ideas that need only to be shaped into acceptable final form. Rather, writers begin with an empty page and fill that page only as they discover what they think and feel, what they wish to say. This process of discovery begins with pre-writing, a process in which we examine new information, search back through our own experiences for relevant associations, sort out the values, feelings and ideas we bring to the task at hand. As we engage in pre-writing, we begin to formulate the assertions or hypotheses that will become the substance of an initial draft. Sometimes, pre-writing may take place over a period of days and months; we read, think about and discuss a topic with colleagues long before we actually begin to write about it. But often pre-writing cannot be such a leisurely process. On relatively short notice, we must decide how we think and feel and, hence, what we shall write about a given issue or problem. And sometimes we can't even assume that our topic has been neatly defined for us. We may have to determine for ourselves exactly what the issue is; we may have to define the problem—or even create a problem—in ways that will let us think and write effectively.

Once our pre-writing has allowed us to create an initial draft, the process of discovery has just begun. Donald Murray, a Pulitzer Prize-winning journalist and a student of the composing process, makes the point thus: "Writing is rewriting. Most writers accept rewriting as a condition of their craft; it comes with the territory. Rewriting is the difference between the dilettante and the artist, the amateur and the professional, the published and the unpublished" (Murray, 1975). By *rewriting*, Murray has in mind something much more basic than editing our work to make sure we've observed conventions of form and usage. When Murray talks of rewriting, he is referring to a continued process of discovery in which we make substantial changes in the initial draft, relating ideas in the draft to new information, re-thinking our initial sense of what our topic is, how we feel about it, and what we're trying to accomplish by writing about this topic. Occasionally—Murray cites several examples—a writer's first draft needs little work; in our first effort, we discover what our topic is, how we feel about it, what we wish to say. But more often the initial version of a piece of writing is little more than a starting point; sometimes the value of a first draft is simply that it helps us see what we do *not* mean to say.

Until the mid 1960s, the processes of pre-writing and revising (as opposed to editing) received relatively little attention. Most composition texts were based (as many still are) on a rhetorical theory that is primarily concerned with arrangement and style in the final draft of a written product. Unfortunately, all of the standardized tests we've examined are in large part restricted to the assumptions of this theory. Such a restriction is unjustifiable. We have good theoretical and introspective accounts of the process of discovery (Elbow, 1973; Larson, 1975; Young, Becker and Pike, 1970) as it relates to the process of writing. Further, we have research (Odell, 1974; Young and Koen, 1973) demonstrating that readers can make reliable judgments about writers' use of these processes. The point seems inescapable: the process of discovery is an essential part of the composing process. No test can measure "the full range of skills involved in the process of good writing" unless the test can provide some insight into the processes of discovery, specifically the processes of prewriting.

In addition to their failure to measure the process of discovery, standardized tests exhibit two other deficiencies, both of which were suggested in the previous section of this article. These tests do not measure the full range of choices that writers—including the writers of standardized test manuals and price lists—must be able to make. These tests determine only whether students can make choices on the basis of correctness, conciseness and clarity. They do not allow us to find out whether students can make the more difficult choices that are based not solely on these criteria but on one's sense of purpose in writing and of his sense of his relationship to his audience. Furthermore, standardized tests only measure students' ability to select from among alternatives someone else provides. These tests completely ignore the more crucial issue of whether students can generate— and *then* choose wisely from—their own alternatives.

How Useful Are Standardized
Tests for Diagnosis and Teaching?

Given the argument developed in the preceding section, none of the standardized tests is as useful as it ought to be. Since none deals with the process of discovery or rewriting, none can diagnose students' difficulties with these processes or suggest what students need to do if they are to engage in these processes more effectively. At best, these tests can provide only very limited help with diagnosis and teaching.

McGraw-Hill Basic Skills System Writing Test. Although the *Examiner's Manual* says that the MHBSS is "designed to be diagnostic only in a general way," the test can be of only *very* limited help to teachers and students. Each item in the test is related to materials contained in McGraw-Hill Basic Skills System texts. Results of the test should allow a teacher to identify which McGraw-Hill materials a student should work with in order to "improve skills and overcome deficiencies." The very limited nature of the test, however, restricts the kind of help it can provide. As we tried to show earlier, there are important composing skills that the test does not examine and, presumably, that materials in the composing textbooks do not teach. To state our conclusion more generally, we can say that the MHBSS has content validity but lacks construct validity; that is, it tests what the McGraw-Hill Basic Skills System texts claim to teach, but it does not test what we know to be basic in the composing process. But even as a content-valid test to be used with specific materials, the MHBSS appears to have the wrong basic design: It should be criterion-referenced rather than norm-referenced.

Sequential Tests of Educational Progress: Writing. The *Manual* for STEPW contains a numbered list of "uses" of the test. We want to present the entire list here because it illustrates the inflated claims test publishers often make:

1. Identifying a student who is especially advanced or retarded in writing abilities.

2. Comparing a student's writing ability, as measured by STEP WRITING, with his achievement in English courses and other school courses which demand a great deal of writing—in order to identify and help the over- or under-achiever.

3. Giving parents a realistic and straightforward estimate of a student's developed ability in writing.

4. Guiding a student toward verbal or non-verbal academic goals and courses by encouraging him to consider his present developed writing abilities in making academic plans.

5. Suggesting the level of instruction in writing which is appropriate to an individual student in an English class.

6. "Grouping" students of roughly similar levels of ability in writing for some instructional purposes in the English class.

7. Studying development of a student's writing ability over a period of years.

8. Comparing a student's developed ability in writing with his reading and listening comprehension abilities in order to get an over-all picture of his development in the communication skills.

The above are grand and comprehensive claims, but they are not supportable, since the test lacks content and construct validity, as we have shown. The test does not quite measure what it says it measures, and it most certainly does not measure what the best current theory and research tell us about the unique construct "composing a piece of writing." Notice how the term "writing ability" is used now in a global way in each of the eight uses. The test sellers clearly intend the score on STEPW to be taken for measure of "writing ability."

Since it treats "writing ability" as a single global construct, STEPW provides almost no help with problems of diagnosis and teaching. The *Manual* claims that items in the test can be classified "on the basis of the major responses they demand." That is, authors of the test were able to determine whether a given item tested a student's ability to think critically, organize reasonably, observe conventions, etc. However, results of the test appear as a single score, which gives no clue as to specific area (critical thinking, etc.) in which a student might need help. Moreover, even if results were reported on specific areas identified in the *Manual*, those results—since they are derived from an unjustifiably limited test—could provide only a partial understanding of a student's skill in writing.

As the *Manual* points out, students' scores on the STEPW will give us a normative rank-ordering for a group of students, and we can then use that information for teaching or grouping. However, there is no evidence that such groupings are essential for writing improvement.

Missouri College English Test. Like the MHBSS and the

STEPW, the MCET gives us a single normative score for each student. We could raise the same questions we have discussed above about the usefulness of this score. Since these three standardized tests are representative of all such tests available for purchase, we must conclude that they are of almost no help to anyone and therefore are not worth the expense. Wasted educational funds aside, however, the most serious problems with the tests is that they mislead teachers and students and unnecessarily limit our understanding of composing and its teaching.

Must We Use Standardized Tests in Order to Have Reliable Measures of Writing Performance?

In spite of all we have said above, one might still defend standardized writing tests by arguing that they are objective and fair. But we do not believe such an argument is presently convincing. As briefly as possible here, we will try to outline our reasons.

Recent research and development in measurement demonstrates that we can achieve reliable and objective measures of nearly all the important features of a piece of writing. Since these features are so centrally important in judgments of the quality or maturity of a piece of writing, the judgments bring us much closer to useful inferences about a writers' control of various stages in the composing process. In short, we know that human readers can make reliable judgments and develop reliable descriptions of crucial aspects of actual pieces of writing.

The much-touted unreliability of human raters, their lack of agreement about grades or scores on papers, is a function of the specificity and clarity of scoring criteria and the amount of training. If raters have similar backgrounds and a brief period of training (two or three hours) with clear scoring criteria, they can cooperatively achieve high reliability (above .90) of judgment about a student's writing ability, where they have the time to provide for each paper four independent ratings requiring less than two minutes each. A number of recent researchers (Cooper, 1975; Diederich, 1974) have outlined plans for teachers to follow in organizing and training themselves to achieve reliable writing scores for an entire student body, grade level or entering/existing group. Furthermore, recent research on syntactic fluency (Christensen, 1967; Hunt, 1965) and writing strategies (or intellectual strategies) (Odell and Cooper, in press) has brought us to the stage of precision where nearly perfect rater agreement is possible.

We should caution that these procedures take time and that they must be made on at least two pieces of writing from each student, to insure a reliable sample of the student's writing performance. However, money saved on standardized tests can be used to buy time to carry out the procedures we are recommending. But whatever the loss in time, anyone familiar with the composing process and the nature of written products would have to conclude that careful holistic judgments and descriptive procedures carried out on actual pieces of writing are the only way to obtain valid measures of writing. Furthermore, we have just shown that these measures can be as reliable as the scores on standardized tests.

To carry this line of argument one step further, we would like to point out that the one writing skill—editing—that present standardized tests do appear to be measuring is just the one narrow skill for which teachers can design their own highly reliable tests. We would recommend that where teachers feel the need for them—and we would acknowledge the need, particularly since there are now available programmed workbooks for capitalization, punctuation, spelling and correct usage—that they design their own separate tests of 30 or 40 items for each editing skill. Any teacher's handbook on test construction outlines simple procedures for item analysis and computing reliability, which can easily be in the mid-90s on such a teacher-made test.

The generally negative answers to questions we've raised throughout this analysis of a few writing skills tests lead us to pose one final question. Is it reasonable to expect that standardized tests will ever provide significant information about students' writing ability? It would be nice if our answer could be an unequivocal affirmative.

If these tests were construct-valid, they would provide teachers a quick and easy way to assess students' skill as writers. But given the theoretical assumptions and the multiple choice format of tests, the only answer we can give is *No*. Rhetorical theory and research in the process of composition make it clear that information derived from standardized tests of writing is unjustifiably limited. We cannot assume that results of these tests provide a basis for discussing students' writing ability. So long as we make such an assumption, our discussions will continue to generate much heat and very little light indeed.

Recommendations for Development
of Tests and Treatments

An extension of some of the above analysis provides a useful takeoff for formal recommendations. There has been a decline in writing skills test scores over the past decade. The decline is real. What are some of the possible causes of the decline? See Table 1.

Since the present data do not allow clear statements as to the amount of decline in writing skills performance, due to the variables summarized above, some analysts have suggested the implications for research to provide a data base for interpretation of the decline. This is excellent. But the problem remains, and schools will test and teach. Focus attention instead on directions for program development assuming the complex of forces outlined above are operating somehow to lower writing skills test scores. It is clear that in a given school or program or class or for a given child one might, without much difficulty, identify at some useful level the kinds of variables outlined above as contributors to the test score decline in writing skills. Use that summary as a kind of checklist. Also assume that the decline is significant, the skills of high priority and the value of correcting the deficiencies worth the cost. It would not be very difficult to propose procedures for

Table 1

Summary of Some Possible Causes of
Decline in Writing Skills Test Scores

The Person: Who is being tested?	Interference: Competing peer activities	Doing Writing: Time allocation to writing within the school	Consequences: Teacher/Parent feedback and provisions of contingencies for performance
1. The persons tested represent an increasingly wider range of ability because of the reduction in drop-out rate.	1. Peer group involvement of some students in drug abuse, alcohol consumption and youth crime provide strongly reinforced activities competing with writing.	1. Absence rate increase reduces time for writing.	1. More independent study and student scoring of own work yield less accurate and less specific feedback on formal aspects of writing.
2. Major cultural changes have produced many persons with stable (not easily environmentally controlled) disinterest in formal writing tasks.	2. Peer group involvement in within-school and out-of-school activities beyond the "basics" in writing (music, art, sports, leadership, vocations) draws time away from basics.	2. Declining course enrollment in English in secondary schools reduces number of persons taking writing skills courses.	2. Less homework yields less parent feedback on specifics of performance.
		3. Changes in curriculum allow more free time (independent study) often not used for academics and more emphasis on individual written expression and oral communication with a sacrifice in formal writing.	3. Changes in family yield less attention to children by adults (children born closer together, fewer adults in home, more working parents, more single-parent families).

program development to correct the deficiencies identified for a given student, class or program. For deficiencies in motivation, introduce incentives. For deficiencies in frequency, accuracy and specificity of corrective feedback on student writing, introduce clear checklists or guides for teacher (teacher aide, student) analysis of writing performance. And so on. These things must certainly be done and school program personnel may well use the help of educational technologists in the analysis of such deficiencies, the design of appropriate solutions and the implementation and follow-up evaluation of changes introduced. But while current programs are going on, there is the pressing question of assessment procedures for program evaluation. The evaluation for a small class or school is one thing. Large scale evaluation is another.

Let's now focus more narrowly on some directions for development of more adequate assessment measures. After all, if the variables outlined above could be influencing test performance, we really do not know what is represented by test scores. Add to this the evidence that test scores do not appear to be highly related to out-of-class writing success and one develops even more interest in the problems of assessment of writing skills.

Turn attention away from the test score decline issue to the test score itself. Tests *are* being used for selection of students into programs, classification into special treatments, judgment of writing for publication or other kinds of merit, judgments of programs, and even substitution for courses and high school graduation requirements.

Consider a test task as simple as writing a letter of thanks to the school custodian for the work he does. What are some of the plausible ways in which we may *account for* differences in performance with respect to numbers of words, syntactic complexity and originality (unusual or interesting content or style)? Following is a quickly generated brief listing:

Some Possible Ways of Accounting
for Individual Responses on a
"Write a Letter" Task

1.   The person may be making a recently determined or strong pre-existing response literally borrowed from what one has read or heard.
2.   The person may be responding to a formal prompt for a type of *exercise* previously engaged in and practiced.
3.   The person may find the test instructions discriminative for a response deemed useless or insincere and may try to ruin the test by an irrelevant response.
4.   The person may generate many responses that are sincere and formally correct but censor them because of social norms.
5.   One person may find the instructions discriminative for a one sentence "thank you" while another assumes the instructions are discriminative for a full page "thank you."
6.   The person may make a response never before made by himself (or heard in that chain or sequence, or read) through a complex chain of intraverbal associations.
7.   The person may discriminate letter writing as a three-phase task (talk it out, write a draft, revise) and get instead a one-phase task—write it.

The possibilities are limitless. The point is clear. What does a test score mean? For the technologist many of the problems of assessment of writing skills implied in the above list can be solved by getting an adequate baseline (enough testing occasions and topics to get a reliable maximum performance estimate). But there is another important consideration that will require considerable developmental work prior to the production of even a draft of a formal test. We suggest below the essence of what is required for adequate analysis of writing skills *prior to* formal test development.

For a more comprehensive treatment of these issues consult the paper on "Research Strategies for the Study of Revision Processes in Imaginative Writing" (Della-Piana, 1975). The major consideration is as follows.

There is a large body of data in available documents that could inform the test developer (and program developer) concerning developmental stages in reaching maturity in a particular kind of writing and concerning actual writing and revision processes. Whether the writing of concern is business letter writing, editorial writing, poetry, short story or informal communication, a large body of data is already available. An analysis of such documents would certainly provide a realistic picture of how writing *does* get done and what course of development it follows. The available documents would include theories of rhetoric and prosody, notebooks of writers, revision manuscripts, business office files, biography, autobiography, writers describing their own writing, and teachers' descriptions of writing.

Structured observations of writers at different kinds of tasks might also inform the program developer and evaluator concerning writing processes. The time spent, the conditions under which writing is accomplished, the ways in which one prompts or cues or stimulates one's own writing, the use of audience reaction (others and oneself), the obstacles to development of performance, are all matters essential to an analysis of writing *prior to* the development of new assessment procedures and program interventions.

It is possible that writing processes may not be known nor knowable. But standardized tests are being used *as if* one knows. An examination of the data sources suggested above may inform the technologist in ways that lead to quite unpredictable successes and failures in test making and program development.

References

Advisory Panel to Assess Causes of Decline in SAT Scores. *The College Board News*, January 1976, 4(2), 1, 5.

Callis, R. and W. Johnson. *Missouri College English Test*, Forms A and B and Manual. New York: Harcourt, Brace and World, 1965.

Christensen, F. *Notes Toward a New Rhetoric*. New York: Harper and Row, 1967.

Cooper, C.R. Measuring Growth in Writing. *English Journal*, March 1975, 64, 111-120.

Daniels, H. Viewpoint: What's New with the SAT? *English Journal*, September 1974, *63*, 11-12.

Della-Piana, G. Research Strategies for the Study of Revision Processes in Imaginative Writing. Paper presented at the 1975 Buffalo Conference on Researching Composing, State University of New York at Buffalo.

Diederich, B. *Measuring Growth in English*. Champaign, Illinois: National Council of Teachers of English, 1974.

Educational Testing Service. *Sequential Tests of Educational Progress: Writing*, Forms IA and IB and Manual. Princeton, New Jersey: Educational Testing Service, 1957.

Elbow, P. *Writing Without Teachers*. New York: Oxford University Press, 1973.

Ferguson, R.L. and E.J. Maxey. *Trends in the Academic Performance of High School and College Students*. ACT Research Report No. 70. Iowa City, Iowa: The American College Testing Program, 1976.

Harnischfeger, A. and D. Wiley. Achievement Test Scores Drop. So What? *Educational Researcher*, 1976, *5*(3), 5-12.

Hunt, W. *Grammatical Structures Written at Three Grade Levels*. Champaign, Illinois: National Council of Teachers of English, 1965.

Larson, L. Discovery Through Questioning: A Plan for Teaching Rhetorical Invention. In W. Ross Winterowd (Ed.) *Contemporary Rhetoric: A Conceptual Background with Readings*. New York: Harcourt, Brace, Jovanovich, 1975.

Maxwell, J.C. National Assessment of Writing: Useless and Uninteresting? *English Journal*, 62, 1973, 1254-1257.

Munday, L.A. *Declining Admissions Test Scores*. ACT Research Report No. 71. Iowa City, Iowa: The American College Testing Program, 1976.

Murray, D.M. Internal Revision: A Process of Discovery. Paper presented at the 1975 Buffalo Conference on Researching Composing, State University of New York at Buffalo.

National Assessment of Educational Progress. *Writing Mechanics, 1969-74*. Report No. 05-W-01. Washington, D.C.: U.S. Government Printing Office, 1975.

Odell, L. Measuring the Effect of Instruction in Pre-Writing. *Research in the Teaching of English*, Summer 1974, *8*, 228-240.

Odell, L. and C.R. Cooper. Describing Responses to Works of Fiction. *Research in the Teaching of English*, in press.

Raygor, A. *Writing Tests*, Forms A and B and Examiner's Manual, (McGraw-Hill Basic Skills System). Monterey, California: CTB/McGraw-Hill, 1970.

Slotnick, H.B. On the Teaching of Writing: Some Implications from National Assessment. *English Journal*, 62, 1973, 1248-1253.

Young, R. and F.M. Koen. *The Tagmemic Discovery Procedure: An Evaluation of Its Uses in the Teaching of Rhetoric*. Project Report, Grant No. EO-5238-71-116. Washington, D.C.: National Endowment for the Humanities, 1973.

Young, R.E., A.L. Becker and K.L. Pike. *Rhetoric: Discovery and Change*. New York: Harcourt, Brace and World, 1970.

14.

The Test Score Decline: Are the Public Schools the Scapegoat?

Carmelo V. Sapone and
Joseph R. Giuliano

Recently, the American public schools have undergone severe criticism of their accomplishments and of the increased funds necessary to maintain quality education. Hard-line critics have launched a massive attack on many of the assumptions and practices held by modern-day educators. They have cited evidence of failure in areas usually held sacrosanct and have expressed widespread alarm at the decline of a series of test scores, most notably in the Scholastic Aptitude Test (SAT), commonly known as the "College Boards."

The declining scores provide an easy rationale for broadly condemning the public schools—making them the scapegoat and thereby avoiding the need to carefully study the entire phenomenon. Thus, statements such as "let's return to the basics," or "let's do it the way we used to run the schools" provide *the answer* to the test score decline dilemma. Our schools deserve more thoughtful appraisals.

This article will address itself to the following issues:

- The reasons for the decline of test scores.
- A defense of public education.

Carmelo V. Sapone is Superintendent of Schools, and Joseph R. Giuliano is Educational Consultant, New Hampshire Supervisory Union 29, Keene, New Hampshire.

Reasons for the Decline
of Test Scores

After viewing the literature on the causes of the decline, the authors have concluded that the following complex factors offer possible (and only *possible*) clues:

1. Recent curricular changes, made in response to social needs, are likely to be partially responsible for test score decline in some subject areas.

2. Districts and schools, as well as classrooms, have experienced massive organizational change.

3. Test score declines observed in the upper grade student population could be partially attributed to compositional changes in secondary school student retention.

4. The average number of days attended per enrolled pupil has dropped, due to higher absence rates, resulting in smaller average amounts of schooling for pupils.

5. The proportion of pupils in academic courses has decreased at every grade level.

6. A total drop of almost 11 percent in English enrollments in a two-year period is a probable and startling cause of verbal score declines.

7. There has been an enrollment decline of 7.5 percent in high school foreign language.

8. History enrollments, although not changed measurably, have been redistributed markedly. Regular history course selection has declined by six percent.

9. The total number of courses per pupil in mathematics has decreased from 0.768 to 0.713, a total drop in enrollment of more than seven percent in two years.

10. Course enrollments in the natural sciences in 1970-71 and 1972-73 have decreased consistently in general science (grades 7-12); biology (first year); chemistry (first year); and in physics (first year).

11. A 1973 Gallup Poll, which assessed public attitudes toward "The Importance of Education to Success," showed that

the rate of endorsement of this concept increased with age. Students currently in school do not strongly support this concept.

  12. The current teaching force as a whole, though better qualified, is less experienced than that of the 1960s.

  13. Teacher mobility (defined as the proportion of the teaching staff leaving a school per year) might be an indicator of pupil outcomes.

  14. Course enrollment declines parallel closely the test score decline patterns.

  15. TV ownership and the amount of time that families spend viewing television has continually increased, including the period of the test score decline. (This was true until 1976, when a six percent decline in TV viewing occurred.)

  16. The National Institute on Drug Abuse (NIDA), reports that eight- to fourteen-year-olds constitute the fastest growing group of drug users.

  17. Large increases in the proportion of working mothers result in less time being spent in family relationships.

  18. The number of illegitimate children has climbed precipitously—the percentage of such births more than tripling between 1948 and 1974.

  19. Perhaps one of the most promising hypotheses about the test scores decline is found in the work of Robert B. Zajonc.* His thesis is that the test score decline is directly related to birth order and family size. It appears that later-born children, especially those from large families, tend to have lower intellectual ability than first born. The authors believe that Dr. Zajonc has hit on the simplest and perhaps most important cause of the mysterious decline in SAT scores. SAT scores reached a peak in the early 1960s, when many of the students taking the test were first- and second-born children born during World War II. The average scores began to drop as their brothers and sisters—offspring of the "baby

*Family Configuration and Intelligence, *Science*, April 1976, *191*(16), 227-236.

boom" of the late 1940s and the 1950s—entered the college market. The decline in SAT scores, in other words, directly reflects the increased family size of the post-war years and the students' later-birth orders. With the return to smaller families, then, the test scores might begin to climb once again.

A Defense of Public Education

Within the last two hundred years of this nation, our public schools have been called upon, and been expected to respond to, the needs and expectations of a social order that has been marked by change so continuous, so rapid and so extensive as to retard and, in many ways, nullify the role of traditional education.

In one of the most extensive research studies of alternatives and teaching innovations of the past two decades—team teaching, nongrading, open space, etc.—writers Lyn S. Martin of the University of Connecticut and Barbara N. Pavan of Temple University report in the January, 1976 issue of *Phi Delta Kappan* that these innovations may not be doing much good, but certainly are doing no harm. These writers studied dozens of research reports on nongrading, heterogeneous grouping, open space and team teaching; and, although the research proved divergent, often conflicting and never conclusive, they found it led to "meaningful conclusions," if not to "unquestioned truth."

They found that the new techniques "do not," either alone or in combination, result in detrimental effects on cognitive or affective outcomes. Their research indicates that, when properly interpreted and implemented, these innovations may be a step toward educational improvement and are, in any case, valid alternatives.

According to a nationwide study made by National Assessment for the Right to Read Effort of the U.S. Office of Education, two percent more 17-year-old students in 1974 could answer basic reading questions correctly than 17-year-old students in 1971.

CEEB President Sidney P. Marland, Jr. states that there is no substantial evidence that enables us to attribute the SAT score decline to any single cause or any particular set of causes. To single out the schools as being responsible for the decline is unwarranted, unfair and scientifically unfounded, states Marland. Marland also stresses that the SAT is not a measure of school performance alone, but also includes skills acquired *outside of schools*.

Many sociologists and psychologists today have concluded that there is a high and significant relationship between academic success and parent interest and involvement with their children in school affairs. It is believed that parental attitude does have significant effects on the ability of children to benefit from formal educational experiences.

Today's decline in standardized test scores may then, in fact, reflect the attitudes of parents toward their schools, their children and today's society. It may also reflect the influence of television, permissive parents or dozens of factors *beyond the control of the schools*.

Education, today, is also a victim of social unrest. This may be due to our recent economic problems and the policies of our states and federal government.

Still, among the population 25 to 29 years old, the proportion of those who have graduated from high school has risen from 60 percent to 80 percent in the past 14 years.

Other evidence dramatically shows that more students are enrolling in institutions of higher learning, both in two- and four-year schools.

More books are being published and read by students than in the past. Library statistics show increases in the circulation of books as well as tapes, slides, filmstrips, records and other audio-visual materials.

The truth of this confusing issue of declining test scores, we believe, is that students today are learning more, reading more, writing better, participating in postsecondary education and remaining in school longer than students of the past.

Conclusion

These authors conclude that citizens of our society will soon realize that our schools are currently performing *better* than in the past. An improvement in *support* of our schools is in order.

15.

You Can Lead the Public to Educational Technology But You Can't . . .

George L. Gropper

There is still not enough "technology" in educational technology. An instructional designer or a teacher with a particular objective to teach cannot go to a handbook and find an undisputable prescription for it. Fortunately, no one of us is being called upon to build an Eiffel Tower. For what we might be asked to do, our expertise is technologically adequate today and time alone will be needed to make it more than just adequate.

The lack of full-fledged maturity, the absence of iron-clad prescriptions, is insufficient reason not to take advantage of what educational technology can do now. Even when it is indifferently applied, its built-in provisions for empirical self-correction assure higher levels of student achievement than less self-conscious approaches to instruction can produce. Why, then, with the continued anxiety and perplexity about why Johnny can't read, write or add up a column of figures is educational technology, which has the potential for dealing with these problems, making so little headway in the educational market-place? The question takes on additional importance as the concern about the declines in SAT and ACT scores begins to grow.

George L. Gropper is Coordinator for Instructional Design, Project on the Design and Management of Instruction, University of Pennsylvania, Philadelphia.

An observer of the scene can more readily point to reasons for the problem than to methods for its solution: There is widespread and palpable indifference and even hostility to educational technology; its products are arguably effective and efficient; and the cost of producing them is unarguably high. Let us take each in turn.

The Unreceptive Audience for
Educational Technology

The variable reception educational technology has received is in part traceable to prevailing attitudes to "education" generally. It is no state secret that "educationist," particularly at colleges and universities, is a pejorative word. Educational technology has inherited the scorn that has so often been visited on its in-laws who have been so labeled. No matter that there has been a healthy and sizable infusion of research-based learning principles, and no matter that learning and training psychologists have in the main shaped the field, educational technology arrived on the scene predestined, at best, to be ignored and, at worst, to be derided.

Members of some disciplines, particularly those in the humanities and in some of the social sciences, raise objections to the rhetoric of educational technology, to its methods of analysis, or to the theory supporting it. "Maybe all this applies to other fields; but it's not appropriate to mine." "Systems language is not graceful enough." "The analysis of subject matter is reductionist and destroys the true, holistic character of the discipline." "An S-R approach is mechanistic and therefore guarantees the pursuit of trivial educational goals." No matter that educational technologists encourage the disciplines to state their *own* goals, however complex or demanding. While educational technologists must demonstrate that they can indeed apply their models to such goals, the disciplines have not been eager hosts for the necessary, appropriate test.

The reasons for resistance to educational technology are

often more directly personal. No one, whether at the college level or at the elementary grade level, wants to give up a job to a shelf full of stored materials. No matter that educational technologists have identified roles for teachers more appropriate than their current role as presentors of expository material. No one wants to dwell on his lack of preparation to teach or on the variable results his teaching (prepared or unprepared) produces or to expend the effort needed to master a new, if as yet insufficiently proven, approach which might provide the necessary preparation. No matter that opportunities have been created to help in learning about and in implementing educational technology. Perhaps most critical of all, no one wants to give up the prerogative of doing one's own thing with one's own course. No matter that an integrated and appropriately sequenced curriculum clearly depends on collegiality both within and across disciplines.

Not least among the reasons for the resistance to educational technology is lack of adequate knowledge about it. Faculty or administrators in public or private schools at all levels may never have heard of educational technology (or some of the synonyms for it including: instructional technology, instructional development, instructional design, or the systems approach), or they may confuse it with the use of hardware (cassettes, closed-circuit TV, projectors, etc.), or they may mistakenly believe, often with great conviction, that conventional instruction does much if not all of what educational technologists say *they* do.

Characteristics of Available
Educational Technology Products

From the outside looking in, educational technology could be seen as nothing more than the latest in a series of fad solutions to the problems of education. After all, there are in education itself people who are for it and people who are against it. Even among those who are for it, there is a Babel of voices as to what it is and how it must be applied. Are there any agreed-on principles, procedures, standards?

There are hundreds of products on the market. Some look like one another and different from conventional products. Others look like conventional products but the labels say otherwise. Some do seem to have trivial goals. Some do seem to contribute to the blur between the software technology (i.e., educational technology) and the hardware technology. A filmed lesson, conventional in every way, may be advertised as the product of educational technology. How is the potential buyer to make the necessary distinctions?

The people who attempt to market the new products also market the old. The prestige of a publishing firm is used to back one as much as the other. How is the potential buyer to make the necessary distinctions?

Can the products themselves be indicted for the hostility or the indifference they experience out there? Clearly there is no product currently available that is capable of doing for reading, or for writing, or for quantitative skills, the high-visibility problem areas in education, what medicine has done for curing disease or what engineering has done for improving construction. Even today, for all its immaturity, educational technology has the potential for that kind of coup. Why hasn't it pulled it off?

Anyone who is puzzled about the failure of educational technology to conquer the marketplace need only inspect available products: for the goals their developers seek to attain, for the manner in which they go about developing products suitable to those goals, for the ways the products so developed do or do not deal with issues of student motivation and individual differences, or for the compensations for past student learning failures the products must incorporate.

1. *Educational Goals*

The goals of much of what is available in the educational technology marketplace are indeed trivial. Factual recall is overstressed. The developers of such materials should, however, be faulted on that score no more or no less than those who produce conventional materials or who give conventional presentations (i.e., lectures). Much of what goes on in the classroom also overemphasizes recall of factual material. Since the classroom teacher or the college faculty member typically serves as subject matter expert for the educational technologist, it should hardly come as a surprise that the goals of an innovative as well as of a conventional mode of instruction should have so much in common.

It may well be that by concentrating solely on the formal properties of how objectives are stated and by politically and defensively deferring to subject matter specialists for curriculum decisions, the educational technologist has acquiesced in the perpetuation of poorly conceived goals. In what sense poorly conceived? It is very easy for a grade school teacher or a college faculty member to think back to the education he received in his discipline or to inspect the table of contents in available texts in that discipline (however much admired) and to leap to the conclusion that that represents what a field is all about. In contrast, it takes special training to be able to determine *how one would go about* deciding in systematic ways what competencies the graduate of a course or of a program ought to have. Small wonder that there are so many so-called innovative programs (whether in professional schools, in graduate schools, in undergraduate colleges or in elementary or secondary grades) that stress not only the recall of factual knowledge but also other competencies not remotely related to or required for successful post-program performance. Small wonder that there are few programs that self-consciously seek to identify new, more demanding and both intellectually and socially more justifiable goals.

2. *Approaches to Development*
The more time and effort spent on developing educational

products, and presumably the more systematic and analytic its expenditure, the leaner and more efficient, as well as more effective, the product that is likely to result. While product development is, it is admitted, the result of both method and of intuition, the balance in much of current developmental efforts seems to favor intuition. This is the case not only in initial development but also in empirical tryout and revision. There is considerable variation among educational technology practitioners as to the degree of expertise they bring to their work. This is understandable. The field is young. There is no accreditation. Its methods and its standards are still under development. It is easy for practitioners whose expertise is in other disciplines to adopt surface attributes of the technology. So, for example, despite the fact that there is evidence that indicates that the particular response selected for students to fill in is critical for effective learning, there are programmed texts in which the blank to be filled in appears to have been selected in a rather arbitrary manner. (See later for further comment on requiring students to fill in blanks.) When such is the case, product effectiveness and efficiency can only suffer. Thus, educational technology is unfortunately resisted by some and, just as unfortunately, too quickly and inexpertly accepted by others.

3. *Student Motivation*

Many educational technology products, addressed to well conceived or poorly conceived goals, are longer and more time-consuming than they need to be. This makes them less efficient and potentially more boring than they ought to be. It is an outcome to be expected when the development of commercial products is not based on a systematic, analytic approach to instructional design.

The length of instructional programs, the time and effort it takes to complete them, is apt to distract from student work habits or from student interest in subject matter (and certainly less apt to build such interest if it were not there to begin with) or from interest in learning itself. Perhaps more detrimental to student motivation are substantive features of instructional programs themselves. In particular, in the view of at least one observer, there is the ever-present and depressing requirement in many printed programmed texts that the learner *fill in the blanks*. The unrelenting crossword puzzle character of many programs can do nothing but cast a pall. All that could be helped in part by introducing variations in response requirements. True, variation for variation's sake. But the response requirements which are introduced can be made appropriate to learning needs. 'Recognition' practice can be useful for learning discriminations. 'Editing' practice can be useful in those situations where self-correction is an integral part of the criterion situation. A judicious mix of alternative response modes, with each variation rationally justified as serving an appropriate instructional function, could do much to alter public perceptions about programmed materials as well as to deal more adequately with student motivation; with the possibility of making a cumulative learning experience both more effective and efficient.

Make no mistake about it, 'production' responses are clearly what is required in most criterion situations. And, indeed, programs do require the shaping of gradually longer responses. But, is it shaping of a verbal repertoire which is required? Except for the very young, who have not yet learned to juggle words, what most learning goals require is rather the juggling of ideas.

Students must learn to define individual concepts in their own words, or to illustrate them, or must learn to link two or more concepts in their own words, or must learn to solve problems on the basis of the linkages. If anything we would like them to avoid parroting a fixed sequence of words. The early conviction that 'shaping of responses' is what programs must accomplish was correct. But, it mistakenly focused on verbal repertoires per se. No wonder many programs have that rote, mechanical look. No wonder that many programs are indeed monotonous. All this could be reversed if 'shaping' were more usefully applied to the 'manipulation of ideas' as a goal than to the ordering of a particular set of words. For this new, more relevant and more demanding goal other response modes could be strategically selected and used.

Agreeing with the assumption that it is the manipulation of ideas and not just words that is a chief goal of instruction may allow for greater latitude not only with respect to response modes. It could also allow for variations in the size of the unit of practice. It would be possible to move away from sole reliance on the small-step, fill-in-the-blank type frame. It would also allow for the organization of stimulus materials in a way that emphasizes the inspection of relationships between ideas. It would be possible to move away from sole reliance on cues selected to elicit the single response that correctly fits a blank which has been provided.

Variation in response mode or organization of stimulus material alone will not solve the motivation problem. It is clear that we know far less, or give the unmistaken impression of knowing far less, about how to motivate study behavior or about how to create interest in subject matter or in learning itself than we do about how to teach. And, it is certainly true that many if not most educational programs, either through oversight or from an inability to do so, make no provision for 'motivation' at all.

4. *Students' Past Learning History*

The audience for any particular self-contained product or for any larger comprehensive program, whether it is a group of pre-meds, or high school sophomores or fifth graders, brings with it a history of learning successes and learning failures. That fact has consequences not only for current student 'motivation.' The instructional shape any new program takes on must also reflect that fact. It is certainly clear that to a great extent programs prepared for any particular audience have to contend with the cumulative or progressive disabilities the audience brings with it. Current programs are probably longer and less efficient because they must accommodate students who failed to acquire necessary verbal skills, quantitative skills, problem-solving skills, study skills, etc., much earlier in their learning history. And, indeed, it is hard to picture just how different a college freshman program or a sixth grade program might be from existing programs if a developer could assume a history of only past student learning *successes* just in these basic skills. But different they would be. Not having to make up for past learning failure heaped upon past learning failure heaped upon past learning failure, programs might just be shorter, more efficient, and more interesting.

5. *Accommodating Individual Differences*
Provisions for accommodating individual differences typically include: self-pacing; assignments to remedial branches based on pre-, during- or post-program measures; or assignments to alternative, compensatory treatments (which must in any case be accompanied by *some form of criterion treatment.*) Most of these approaches also make for longer, less efficient programs.

The perceptions of potential customers about the products of educational technology are often wide of the mark. But a look from the inside confirms the sources of some of the uneasiness. Some products not only look rote and mechanical; they are rote and mechanical. Some are long and inefficient. Some make no attempt to make learning interesting or to make a particular subject matter interesting. Some ballyhooed as "accommodating individual differences" at best make up for past failures and at most either perpetuate or compound them. Those in the business thus to some extent share in the blame for turning the potential audience for educational technology products into an unreceptive one.

The Cost of Educational
Technology Products

This book is devoted to a "problem." It is therefore appropriate to size up a field, in this instance, "educational technology," and to concentrate on its deficiencies as potential contributors to that problem. It would be unfortunate if the listing of deficiencies were to obscure the achievements of the field or of the effective products it has produced or of its potential. There are good products available.

But, there is no use denying that the better the product the more expensive it is likely to be. The development of good products requires expertise. That costs. The development of good products requires faithful adherence to a comprehensive, systematic and analytic model of development. That costs. It makes little difference which model. Following the detailed prescriptions of most models requires time and that is what makes it cost. The development of good products requires a commitment to evaluation and empirical revision. That costs. It requires more time and it requires repeated publication. If media other than print are involved, the costs of revision are even greater.

The cost of revision is certainly one that can be expected to decline as we get more "technology" in educational technology. True, it will require more costly expertise initially to develop materials. But, the *need for revision* can concomitantly be expected to decline.

Any self-conscious, systematic approach to instruction, good or bad, is likely to cost more than existing intuitive approaches. To win a portion of the educational market, these more costly approaches will have to demonstrate in a very convincing way just how well they can solve important educational problems. They will also have to be cost-effective.

No matter how less costly or how more cost-effective product development becomes, organizations that commit themselves to large-scale capital expenditures need to be reassured that their investment will not be undone by obsolescence. In part, the solution would appear to call for greater public awareness that many fields are relatively unchanging and that the fear of obsolescence is often unrealistic. For those fields or for those portions of fields where some change is indeed realistically to be expected, solutions to obsolescence are possible. Modularization allows for relatively painless replacement of those portions of programs requiring change. Even less painful is the possibility of preparing adjunct materials to bring programs up to date.

Some Solutions

Limitations of space have made shotgun indictments inevitable. However, the presentments have to some extent expanded the coverage by implying some solutions. This final section will offer more explicit, summary recommendations for the rehabilitation of educational technology.

1. *Stage a coup in a high visibility problem area.*

What is more likely to put educational technology on the map than a smashing success in teaching Johnny to read, or to write, or to add up a column of figures, or to use effective study skills? There is a huge and ready-made public for such a coup.

There are other equally compelling reasons for focusing on early childhood learning. Successfully teaching these basic skills can be highly generative. Since all subsequent learning depends on them, they are essential to any future cumulative history of learning successes.

An approach which guarantees the successful mastery of basic skills can also contribute to a *reduction* in differences among students as opposed to an approach which uses alternative treatments for differently prepared students. This latter approach is in the main remedial in nature and by definition less efficient.

Some personal candidates for basic skills to be taught: Study skills are useful not only when teachers provide all, much, or just some of the instructional input students may receive. They are also useful when students study and learn on their own both in school and beyond school. One way to assure a capacity for this needed, self-reliant learning is to teach students some of the task analysis strategies which instructional designers employ. Taught to be able to identify the types of learning involved in particular types of objectives and taught to be able to identify the types of information needed for those types of learning, students can be prepared to adopt appropriate information search strategies. For example, when learning classifications they would systematically look for information that could help them decide what the criteria are for class inclusion or class exclusion. When learning rule-following procedures they would systematically look for information that could help them identify the sequence of steps involved in the procedures. With the knowledge that such skills are at students' disposal, use of phrases like "active learning" and "self-instruction" would take on more relevant meaning.

What can be done about "reading"? A personal hunch, with no particular expertise or experience to support it, is that reading (perhaps just some of its component skills, e.g., decoding) should be learned at the same time a child learns to talk. Picture each child's crib or playpen with its own portable TV. Picture a child exposed to an object and a word on the screen and a voice saying the word. Picture a parent periodically scripted into the act saying the same word and, when appropriate, reinforcing the child for saying or reading the same word. Picture a parent trained to rely on reinforcment for success and to avoid aversive responses to failures. Picture a child being repeatedly reinforced not only for specific responses but also more generally for active responding. Picture a child not interpreting active responding as a test.

Videocassettes or broadcast TV could be programmed to provide a total, cumulative learning experience based on such interchanges. The goal would be to facilitate learning to read as well as learning to speak. Needless to say, this would be one educational technology product that would also cost. But, if it worked, it would be one cost the public might be willing to bear cheerfully.

2. Attack the motivation problem head on.

There is ample evidence of differential sub-culture support for education being passed from generation to generation. Parental involvement in instruction of their own children, either in the reading plan outlined above or in any other plan, is therefore an important goal in and of itself. If parents can be motivated to be intimately involved in the learning experiences their children undergo, that manifest interest in learning may rub off on the children. That on a mass scale may be what is needed to stimulate interest in basic skills, in specific disciplines, or in learning itself.

Another way educational technology can make itself more visible and more highly valued is to attack the motivation problem directly. It need not restrict itself to the particular recommendations outlined above. All that it does need to do, is to select a way that succeeds. There is, after all, all that operant methodology waiting to be used.

3. Motivate the teachers too.

An operant approach to encouraging teachers to use already available educational technology products or in the preparation of them is an appropriate way to deal with the current resistance or indifference to doing so. Educational technologists who work with faculty and who insist that their continued collaboration is contingent on faculty acceptance of a full-fledged, highly systematic development effort or is contingent on the consent and collaboration of total departments demand too much. It makes considerably better sense to be sensitive to what an individual teacher or faculty member is ready to accept now and to be content to move gradually to levels of collaboration which are more demanding. If that means to begin with simply identifying where slides can be purchased, so be it. From there there can be movement to the collaboration with that faculty member on the preparation of his own slides. And then still more technical collaboration on their selection or preparation within a more systematic instructional design framework. Admittedly this proposal dictates a slow process. But it does reflect a conception of behavior change which is both realistic and practical.

Instructional designers can also speed up the movement in this desired direction, that is, greater faculty use of educational technology products or increased faculty involvement in the preparation of such products, or more systematic use of educational technology principles in the preparation of their stand-up classroom presentations, by making available to faculty opportunities to learn *how*. Design of either instructional packages or of work activities could provide the needed, appropriately sequenced learning experience.

4. *Build some old-fashioned P.R. into the diffusion process.*
For some faculty or some administrators, the first task is to make them aware that educational technology exists. For other faculty or administrators what may be needed is to disabuse them of the notion that it is nothing more than the use of hardware (film, TV, cassettes, etc.). It may also mean disabusing them of the conviction that they already do the same things that educational technologists do.

Faculty and administrators need to be able to distinguish between a self-conscious, transferable approach to the instructional process and an intuitive, non-transferable approach. They need to recognize that what makes the educational technology approach transferable is its *commitment to systematic and analytic prescription*. They need to recognize that conscious decisions are made: to match treatments to types of objectives and to types of target audiences; to match media with the treatments chosen as appropriate to particular objectives or particular audiences; to match materials or presentations and their sequence with the response requirements revealed by objectives (in effect not stopping at the internal organization and relationship among inputs made to students—a stimulus orientation); and to match revisions made in materials or presentations with requirements empirically identified during tryouts with actual students. The list of differences between instruction systematically designed and conventionally designed could go on to cite: active responding; self-pacing; criterion-referenced testing; routine diagnosis of student learning problems; etc.

Diffusion can't get anywhere until, as any P.R. man will tell you, there is product identification.

5. *Provide the public with standards.*

When it comes to the marketing of a *particular* product, the educational technologist owes the public a lot *less* P.R. A commitment to "truth in education," aside from its virtue in its own right, should advance the field and its acceptance. A public that is fully informed of standards a product should meet and whether a particular product meets those standards should be in a better position to select from among the array of good and bad available in the marketplace. One successful experience should lead to an occasion or opportunity for another.

What the standards should be, either for products or the developmental process which produces them, is for those in educational technology collectively to decide. One obvious candidate is the collection and publication of empirical data. The public deserves that as a minimum.

6. *Hold down those costs.*

Perhaps most difficult is the costliness of producing educational technology products. Some of the proposals made above in other connections may also contribute to cost reduction. They include, first of all, training teachers to prepare their own materials or presentations. Second, students should be trained early to be self-reliant learners. Accommodating such a target audience ought clearly to be less developmentally demanding. Third, there should be an early focus on basic skills on which all later learning is contingent and, as a result, less need for remediation due to a past history of learning failures. Also, accommodation of a narrower than usual range of individual differences is less likely to require alternative treatments. Fourth, as educational technology becomes more secure, the number of revision cycles required to bring products up to a standard is likely to decline. Fifth, as standards for products become more public, including explicit rationales for media selection, the marketplace may exhibit a heightened judiciousness about the use of the media mix it offers.

Just how much cost reduction these recommendations will produce remains an empirical matter. But it is a matter important to explore if educational technology hopes to win over a hostile or indifferent public.

You can lead the public to educational technology once again, but whether or not it proves as balky as before depends, in part at least, on solutions to problems this article has sought to identify.

Addendum to
"An Exercise in Freedom"

Eric J. Roberts and
David W. Champagne

Toward the close of the report "An Exercise in Freedom," originally published in *Educational Technology* Magazine, we acknowledged one of the limitations of the work in granting that the effects must be observed in greater detail, with more evidence, in more situations before the certainty of the conclusions could be ensured. Since the time of the original publication, more pieces of those kinds of information have become available. Additionally, initial responses to the article have been collected. This opportunity to extend commentary on the original publication is a luxury authors only infrequently enjoy. Besides, no one ever remembers to include everything the first time 'round. With those considerations in mind, we take advantage of this uncommon chance to bolster, extend and defend our earlier work.

In order to do so, we will offer these new thoughts in a somewhat different style. Rather than once again trying to organize from the very beginning a clear, objective and relatively complete explication of an interesting anomaly, we simply choose to pass along some new details in a "Not only that, but . . ." sort of fashion.

The original report and its findings were presented to a colloquium of University of Pittsburgh School of Education faculty and students. Happily, it provoked considerable discussion, much of it empassioned. One especially vocal participant, an educational researcher, charged that the argument was not convincing. If it can be imagined that the drastic drop in SAT scores for the year 1973 is an aberration, he noted, then the thrust of the report's message is weakened considerably. By supposing there was some effect for that year other than the one discussed (which is a real possibility), he insisted that no firm conclusions could be derived. Perhaps. Other researchers have suggested that the figures do stand up under mathematical examination.

The same colleague also was dismayed by the connection he perceived was made between Project IDEA and EQA and SAT scores. While praising the attitudes, efforts and successes of the project, he damned the need that looks to test scores for justification of good work. Schools are not only for achievement scores, he said; those are not the only results sought. Positive changes are worthy all by themselves. And, anyway, he continued, there is no connection between Project IDEA and the scores.

We agree with the primary contention. The contributions to that school as a social system made by Project IDEA easily justify themselves. When it is possible to do something to make a place more comfortable and more enjoyable for the people who live there, that thing should be done. It needs no other justification. The essential benefit of the project was just this kind of improvement. Groups of praiseworthy individuals combined their efforts to do something honorable, they did it, and that's good. But that is not the only lesson to be learned from this experience. While the changes in atmosphere were being implemented, SAT test scores in this community went up, contrary to a national trend. Years of insistent indoctrination in the peculiarities of science prevent us from proclaiming that one change *caused* the other, but they certainly did *accompany* one another.

There is some kind of connection even if we cannot identify it positively. That the two changes occurred together was interesting to us. We wished to share this interesting observation: *In one school environment, teachers risked changing their relationships with students. In that environment, scores went up.* That's all. That, along with a series of questions prompted by it, is all the report offered.

Another attendant of the colloquium praised the project but proposed that the worst thing an educational community can do to students is to treat them inconsistently. By teaching the students in this school that other possibilities exist, whetting their appetites with attractive alternatives to the schooling with which they had learned to cope, and then possibly returning them to traditional roles and patterns of interactions, he said, the school people may have been doing the students more of a disservice than if they had left them alone with their previously effective adaptive behaviors.

The point is one to be considered and, of course, there is no defense. There is possibly, though, an explanation. At the outset of the project, it was not expected that there would be a relapse to old behaviors. It was hoped that the new ways of teaching and behaving proposed in the project would become the norm.

There have been unfortunate circumstances afflicting this school recently, but, having turned in a fresh direction once, and especially having learned the consequences of not maintaining all of the effort—with all of the inherent implications—it is anticipated that the school will pull itself back in the enviable directions of Project IDEA. For example, the school superintendent said that, over the last year, the greatest portion of his time was spent working through a not-directly-instructional crisis. Naturally, time spent in one way cannot be spent in another. And teachers in the district have expressed the opinion that the superintendent is *the* power figure in the district. What was the result of the superintendent's distraction?

At least some faculty came to believe that the goals of Project IDEA were being devalued. The superintendent did not want this attitude to develop, but it did, nonetheless. What developed along with this attitude?

With decreased pursuit of the goals of Project IDEA, 1976 SAT scores dropped almost 70 points, to 379-verbal and 455-math

(834 combined). The school's guidance counselor is not convinced that all of this change should be attributed to the changes from the activities of Project IDEA, saying that this is just one of those classes that is not as accomplished as some others. He also said, however, that changes in scores may have been influenced as the good feelings that accompanied the intervention persuaded more students to take the SAT than otherwise might have been the case. If that is a real effect, SAT scores collected during the intervention should have gone down. If more less-prepared students were taking the tests, the scores should have dropped. But they didn't. They went up. And now they are going back down. He expects that next year they will jump up again. Are the differences in the classes responsible or is it possible that a rise in SAT scores next year will be accompanied by the school's *rededication* to more open and free alternatives to the norms of traditional schooling?

We shall await this much-discussed rededication and observe carefully its effects.

The intervention mattered to students in ways other than those evidenced on tests. That it mattered positively is demonstrated by the dedication of a yearbook to the coordinator of Project IDEA, a man who had little formal relationship to the students. The responsibilities for that program were not his only responsibilities in the district at that time, but all of the pictures included in the dedication show him in those settings, and most of the phrases used to laud him there are derived from that work. The 1976 graduation ceremonies heard the class salutatorian, class valedictorian and district superintendent all speak about the issues and goals of Project IDEA. And during the time of the full-scale implementation of the project's ideas, there was no appreciable vandalism. But, last winter, when so many of the faculty and staff had relaxed their vigilant attendance to these aspirations, a number of people broke into the school late at night and wreaked an estimated $5,000.00 worth of carefully selective havoc.

Obvious targets, like a glass showcase, were ignored. Other things that could not have shown destruction so dramatically, like books in some settings, were destroyed. Presently nothing more than speculation can explain why this vandalism was so selective. But it is not possible to fail to notice that the rooms most damaged were those of the teachers who were known for strictness and reliance on authoritarian attitudes. Some teachers who did not have a positive relationship with students found their rooms in shambles. The rooms next door, where the teachers and students enjoyed the time they spent together, were not touched.

There is more than a suggestion that the vandalism was a clear message, conscious or not, to those who determine this school's policies.

So what does any of this have to do with SAT scores declining? Some of the discussants of this issue apparently subscribe to the funnel philosophy of education, which is to say, they seem to believe that students essentially are receptacles to be filled by teachers dispensing wisdom. We prefer to see the learning process as a considerably less passive series of interactions with environments, materials, other students, teachers and all resources that can be found. From our point of view, the quality of learning, then, must be seen as influenced greatly by the quality of the interactions. As pointed out previously, the quality of the learnings (as reflected by SAT scores in addition to other measures) increased during the times when a sincere campaign to improve the quality of the interactions was receiving its greatest attention.

A building principal in one of the Providence, Rhode Island schools interpreted this to mean that his plan to improve attitudes about school by reorganizing ninth- and tenth-grade students around a house system likely would not be successful unless he also worked to improve the relationships of students, teachers and administrators as they interacted with themselves and with one another. We would agree with that interpretation, and further, applaud it.

These thoughts are similar to the conclusions of Epstein and McPartland in their report, "The Concept and Measurement of the

Quality of School Life."* While their work primarily is a discussion of their development of an evaluation instrument, it includes certain interesting and pertinent ideas about life in schools.

> Student reactions to school are indicators of the quality of school life. Positive reactions to school may increase the likelihood that students will stay in school, develop lasting commitment to learning, and use the institution to advantage. At least, higher satisfaction with school, greater commitment, and more positive student-teacher relationships mean more enjoyable and stimulating hours spent in the compulsory school setting (pp. 27-8).

And hours that are more enjoyable and stimulating most likely will prove more profitable, and that's what it's all about, isn't it?

For specific information, Epstein and McPartland tell us that "control over one's environment is a stronger associate of satisfaction with school than is either self-esteem or self-reliance . . ." (p. 20) and that "feelings of general well-being may be most strongly influenced by the social structure of the school, commitment may be most related to the task structure, and reactions to teachers most related to the authority structure of the school" (p. 25).

These findings are reported from Maryland. Our supportive conclusions were developed in Pennsylvania. A school staff in Rhode Island is beginning to suspect similar notions. There is a national wave of dissatisfaction among parents and school people with the results of students' public education. Almost assuredly, there is as big a wave among students who are dissatisfied with what schools do to them. Perhaps it can be dismissed with Will Rogers' reminder that "They don't make schools like they used to—and never did." Perhaps something can be done. Perhaps something *was* done, in at least one place, for some time. Perhaps it can be done again.

---

*J.L. Epstein and J.M. McPartland. The Concept and Measurement of the Quality of School Life. *American Educational Research Journal*, Winter 1976, *13*(1), 15-30.

The 1976-77 year will see the school that initiated Project IDEA attempting to push, pull, tug, entreat, connive, tempt, manipulate, coerce and positively reinforce themselves back toward the goals they set a few years ago, as described in our original report. It is not now possible to predict with assurance what will happen, but it will be fascinating to watch. It will be a chance, almost, to observe the classic behavioristic-reinforcement studies (i.e., apply treatment; observe effects; remove treatment; determine if effects return to "normal"; reinstitute treatment; observe whether new effect reappears). This intervention was not planned this way, to be sure, but that is the way it happened and it will be exciting to see what occurs.

We know what we would like to happen. So do they. We shall continue to cooperate with one another. They will continue to talk with us because they believe in the ways we have treated them in their school and in print. We will continue to talk with them because they just may be on the verge of something very important.

And we shall see.

Addendum to
"Assessing Educational Attainments"

Roy H. Forbes

In September, 1976, the National Assessment of Educational Progress (NAEP) released findings from its second survey of the reading abilities of American youths, ages 9, 13 and 17. Improvements and declines mixed with "status quo" to reveal some interesting new facts—and to raise subsequent vexing questions.

Contrary to popular opinion, Johnny—and Mary—at age 9 at least, *are* reading better than their counterparts of a few years ago. The NAEP findings show that between its first reading survey taken in 1971 and the second in 1975, nationwide, an estimated 50,000 more 9-year-olds in 1975 were able to respond correctly to a typical reading item than in 1971.

Moreover, National Assessment found that black 9-year-olds, as a group, showed a "dramatic improvement" in reading skills. The average percentage of black 9-year-olds answering reading items correctly increased 4.8 percentage points, while the average reading performance of white 9-year-olds increased by 1.2 percentage points. However, even with the bigger increases in reading skills, black children are still 13 percentage points below their white counterparts in over-all reading levels.

In other results, National Assessment found that:

• Reading performance of 13- and 17-year-olds changed little over the four-year period, although more 17-year-olds in 1975 were able to read basic, everyday items such as a telephone bill or instructions on a can of pet food.

• As a group, girls continue to read better than boys at all age levels.

• While students in the Southeast are still performing below the national level, the Southeast's 9-year-olds show significant gains in reading skills.

More than 63,000 students took part in each reading survey, which measured students' reading abilities in three areas: literal comprehension, inferential comprehension and reference skills.

For assessment purposes, literal comprehension questions asked students to recognize or identify a single fact, incident or idea given in the reading material. Inferential comprehension required picking from a passage some idea that is not explicitly stated. Reference skills items measured specialized reading competencies needed to solve a problem, or—as the NAEP reading report says—skills that "help students read to learn after they have learned to read."

Some statistical specifics by age:

9-year-olds

• Students from affluent urban areas generally continue to perform considerably above the national levels (6 percentage points), while those from low-income urban areas are still 10 percentage points below the national level.

• Children whose parents graduated from high school but had no further education show an increase of 1.4 percentage points in correct responses. For children whose parents had no high school education there is an increase of 2.4 percentage points, but these 9-year-olds are still 8 points below the national level.

• A significant increase of 2.3 percentage points in reading skills was found for children attending schools in areas of less than 25,000 population.

13-year-olds

• In both 1971 and 1975 reading assessments, female

achievement levels remain about 5 percentage points higher than male achievement levels.

• Reading levels for white 13-year-olds are about 17 percentage points higher than those of blacks.

• Regional comparisons: Southeast—about 4 percentage points below the nation; Central—about 3 percentage points above; West and Northeast—about the same as that of the nation as a whole.

17-year-olds (in school only)

• Students in the Southeast region remain about 4 percentage points below the national level of reading performance, while students in the Northeast and Central regions are about 2 points above the national level. Western students are about 1 percentage point below the nation.

• White 17-year-olds are about 19 percentage points above the reading achievement levels of black 17-year-olds.

• Females continue to hold about a 3.5 percentage-point advantage over males.

National Assessment surveys have detected declines in such learning areas as writing and science. Coupled with the nationwide reports of sagging scores on a variety of college entrance tests, we could ask why, then, is reading apparently "bucking the trend"? Does it mean that the downward drift in student competence and skills is being reversed?

The National Assessment role is not to provide the answers. But it can give the facts, and it is a fact that—in NAEP's eight years of collecting education data—students from the Southeast, from low-income urban areas, who are black or whose parents had limited education, have traditionally achieved below the level of their age group.

It is encouraging to see these gaps in reading achievement levels beginning to close at age 9; it is alarming to see the gaps remaining at ages 13 and 17. Perhaps the improvements found in 9-year-olds' reading skills indicate that special programs at the elementary level are paying off.

With the taxpayers demanding education accountability and a return to the basics, the NAEP data indicate that while we should maintain these programs at the elementary level, attention should also be aimed at the intermediate and secondary schools.